FUN WITH PUPPETS AND SOFT TOYS

by Valerie Janitch

KAYE & WARD · LONDON
in association with Hicks, Smith & Sons
Australia and New Zealand

Contents

(handwritten note in margin: bry to do)

Acknowledgements

The majority of the puppets and soft toys,
and the accompanying illustrations, in this book
are reproduced by kind permission of IPC Magazines Ltd.

First published by
KAYE & WARD LTD
21 New Street, London EC2M 4NT
1974

Copyright © 1974 Kaye & Ward Ltd

ISBN 0 7182 0087 X

Printed in England by Whitstable Litho,
Straker Brothers Ltd, Whitstable.

Introduction

In this book you will find all kinds of puppets and soft toys to make, together with full instructions, patterns, line drawings and photographs to show you how.

The puppets include glove and finger puppets, marionettes, jumping jacks and a very simple cardboard TV puppet with his own appropriate TV setting. Also included is an easy-to-make puppet theatre.

Puppets can be "manipulated" – or worked – in various ways. Glove puppets (like Punch and Judy) are worked by putting your hand inside the body; finger puppets, as the name implies, cover the fingers only. Marionettes have strings which are pulled from above to make the figure move its arms and legs and body. Jumping Jacks are simple, flat puppets which you can cut in thin cardboard to dance on the wall, or act out plays or other entertainments in a model theatre or similar setting.

Creating a character

The soft toys and puppets in this book, although quite different from each other, do have one thing in common: each has a character and personality of its own – whether it is nice or nasty, wise or wicked, kind or evil, funny or sad. This is achieved in a variety of ways: expression, clothes, shape and colour all play a part.

In designing a toy, the best way to achieve the character you want is to study it very carefully before you begin. Find all the references you can, in books, magazines, newspapers, comics, greetings cards, advertisements or on television. Drawings are usually clearer and more helpful than photographs, because an artist tends to exaggerate the most important features of his subject anyway. Comics are often a good place to look – and birthday, Christmas and other greeting cards can be a valuable source of inspiration.

Having collected together all the references you can find, examine everything very carefully and pick out the most telling features which create that particular character – including clothes. Then begin to sketch out the first rough design for your toy, emphasizing and exaggerating whatever you have decided is important to create your particular character: it might be the eyes or the nose or the ears, a funny hat, scruffy hair or baggy trousers . . . It will probably be a combination of several things – but always remember that the best effects are usually achieved by the simplest means: the secret lies in the preliminary research.

Ordinary toys rely entirely on clever design for their personality, but it is easier to give a puppet character, because the animation immediately "brings it to life". So we'll begin by making puppets, and once we have created all kinds of animated characters together, we can investigate the appeal of stuffed toys, and make some attractive examples of those, too.

Brumble Bear: a simple TV puppet

Punch and Judy shows have been making people laugh for many, many years, and in their own way the popular puppet shows on television today carry on this tradition.

Our first puppet is very easy to make. Brumble Bear is a simple flat cardboard figure, but you will see how even a two-dimensional puppet can become an amusing character in the right setting. For Brumble Bear is designed to appear on a miniature TV set. You could call his show "Brumble Bear at Home", because the scenery includes his bed and cooking stove, as well as two tables—one for cooking and one for eating. He has special clothes to wear, too: pyjamas so that he can go to bed—and a chef's hat and apron for when he's trying out new recipes or inventing horrible dishes of his own! You'll notice how his pyjamas make him look sleepy, whilst his chef's outfit gives him a very businesslike air. He also has a telephone, so that he can ring up his friends—and a rabbit which he pulls out of a top hat when he pretends to be a magician . . . and then takes it to bed with him.

You can make the little cut-out figure do all these things and many more, making him seem a very friendly little bear indeed. All you have to do is trace the drawings on to thin card and paper, colour them, cut them out and make up as follows. But just in case you haven't transferred tracings before, here's how it's done.

Transferring tracings

Trace the drawing on to tracing or grease-proof paper.

Rub a soft pencil over the lines on the *back* of the tracing.

Put your tracing in position on the paper on to which you want to transfer the drawing, and go over all the lines again—either with a hard pencil or the point of a knitting needle or something similar.

There will now be a faint black impression of the drawing on your paper: go over the lines again in pencil or ink to make them stronger.

You can use the same tracing over and over again—though you may have to rub your pencil over the back again from time to time.

BRUMBLE BEAR'S TELEVISION SHOW

Materials:

Thin white card
Medium-weight white paper
Copydex adhesive
Paints, crayons or felt pens

Method: Taking care to be *very accurate,* trace the television set on page 5, and the background scenery, the back and front views of Brumble, the rabbit and the telephone on page 7, all on to thin white card. Trace the pyjamas, apron and two hats on to white paper.

Colour the television set and the two tables with their contents. Colour the background scenery in bright colours, too, as well as the clothes, rabbit and telephone—and Brumble himself, who should be golden-brown with darker paws and a pink tongue. To make the outlines stronger, you can go over them again with a fine black fibre-tipped pen.

Cut the television set out very carefully, including the blank area inside the screen, cutting neatly round the articles on the two tables. Then score all the broken lines with a blunt knife, and bend the sides and top, and the tabs, back. Cut out the background scene, slitting the broken line between the

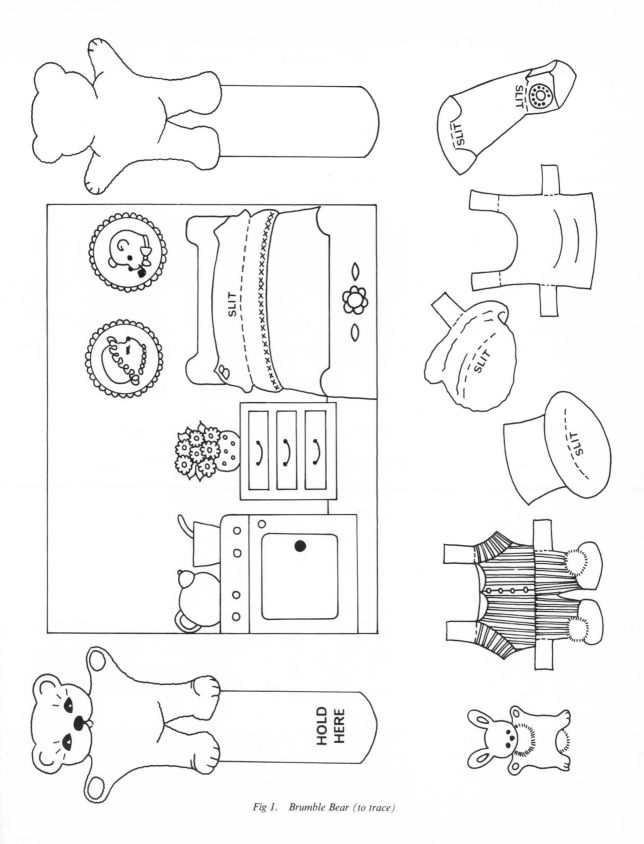

Fig 1. Brumble Bear (to trace)

Brumble Bear

pillow and sheet with a sharp knife. (It's a good idea to ask someone older to do this for you, if you are not used to handling sharp knives).

Now stick the tab at the top of each side under the top of the set, and then stick the three remaining tabs *behind* the background scenery: stick the top edge first, then the sides.

Cut out the back and front views of Brumble, and stick them together. Cut out his clothes, bending the tabs back to hold them in place round his body, and slitting the hats along the broken lines so that they fit over his head and one ear. Cut out the rabbit and telephone: slit the telephone as indicated, so that he can put his paw through the receiver slot, and then slot the telephone over his other shoulder—with the white centre part behind him.

When he goes to bed, Brumble slips *behind* the television set, and pokes up through the slit in the scenery.

6

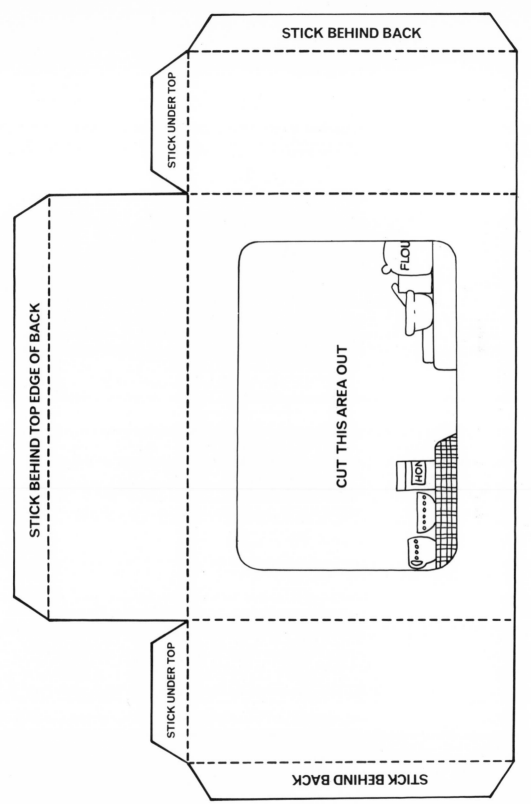

Fig 2. *Brumble Bear TV Theatre (to trace)*

The Puppets of Oakapple Wood: easy-to-make glove puppets

Put your forefinger inside the head, and your thumb and middle finger in the paws—with your two remaining fingers tucked back in the palm of your hand—and you can make these animal glove puppets come to life in a very realistic way. They can wave their paws about, nod and shake their heads excitedly, pick things up or pull them around. The possibilities are endless. And of course, you could write simple plays for them to act. Instructions are given for making a puppet theatre, but you could perform your plays in a converted grocery carton theatre filled with leafy woodland scenery.

The puppets are all made from felt, which is very pleasant to use because it is soft but quite thick and firm, easy to cut and sew, and—best of all—the edges don't fray! And all except Mr Woo, the owl, have exactly the same body pattern—even though they *do* look so different when they are finished.

Compare the pictures and you will see how this difference has been achieved. Apart from colour (which is very important), it is the shape of the face, and the features—the eyes, nose and ears and their positions—which make each character so individual.

Drawing patterns to scale

Before you begin making the Oakapple Wood puppets—and the majority of other designs in this book—you will need to draw the paper patterns to cut your felt or fabric. This is very easy to do from the scale patterns in this book.

Simply rule a sheet of paper into squares the size directed in the instructions (always be extra careful to check the size, because it isn't always the same): better still, use graph paper or pages from a squared exercise book,

but make sure they are the right size.

Then, very carefully, draw the pattern shapes exactly following the lines printed here so that they cross the squares in exactly the same places. When you have finished, you will have a pattern that looks just like the one in this book—but the right size to cut your fabric. Then you can either cut out the pieces you have drawn, or trace them on to grease-proof paper first, to make a thinner pattern.

To make your patterns for the Oakapple Wood puppets: First rule a sheet of paper into **half-inch squares**—or use graph paper. Then draw out your patterns as described, following the appropriate diagrams (Figs. 4, 6, 8, 10, 12 and 13); remember that Cyril, Montgomery, Dominic and the Rabbit Twins all share the same basic body shape.

The features should be traced from the separate diagrams (Figs. 5, 7, 9, 11 and 14).

Make $\frac{1}{4}$in. seams, unless otherwise directed.

CYRIL SQUIRREL

Materials:

12in. square of reddish-brown felt
12in. square of gold felt
Scraps of black and white felt
Reddish-brown double knitting wool
  (about $\frac{1}{2}$oz.)
Kapok for stuffing
2 pipe-cleaners
$\frac{1}{2}$yd. 1in.-wide woven braid
Copydex adhesive

Method: Cut the basic body (Fig. 3) once each in brown and gold, the gusset once and the ear twice in brown, and the head and ear twice each in gold (Fig. 4).

With the right sides together, join the two body pieces, leaving the lower edge open. Trim and clip the seam, and turn on to the right side.

With the right sides together, join the two head pieces between the nose and neck. Now place the pointed tip of the gusset to the top of this seam, right sides together, and join to each side of the head: it is important to do this very carefully, so that the gusset fits accurately and evenly round each side of the head. Clip the seams and turn on to the right side.

Stuff the head firmly and then, with the index finger inside the body, push up into the head and join neatly round the neck, matching the centre front of the neck to the centre front of the body.

To make each ear, join a brown and a gold piece with tiny stab stitches round the outside. Gather the lower edge slightly, and then stitch to the side of the head, following the illustration carefully.

Cut the eyes in white felt, and the pupils and nose in black (Fig. 5). Stick into position as illustrated.

To make his tail, fold a 6in. by 4in. piece of thin card in half lengthways. Now wind the wool round and round it so that you have a series of 2in. long loops. Using a piece of the wool, back-stitch the loops together along the folded edge of the card (avoiding the card), and then cut along the opposite edge. Now place the pipe-cleaners inside, against the centre line of stitches, so that the wool covers about 4½in. of pipe-cleaner: fold over, and oversew the pipe-cleaners firmly into position with the excess at one end.

Make a slit in the back of the body at point X. Push the surplus pipe-cleaners through, bend upwards and stitch them to the inside of the body. Then catch the tail to the body on the outside near the base, so that it stands up firmly instead of flopping down.

Tie the braid round his neck and cut a fringe at each end to make his cosy muffler.

Cyril Squirrel

MONTGOMERY MOLE

Materials:

12in. square of grey felt
12in. square of black felt
Scrap of pale pink felt
Kapok for stuffing
White embroidery cotton
1 artificial rosebud (optional)
Copydex adhesive

Method: Cut the basic body (Fig. 3) once each in grey and black, the gusset once and the ear twice in black, the head twice in grey, and the ear twice more in pink (Fig. 6).

With the right sides together, join the two body pieces, leaving the lower edge open. Trim

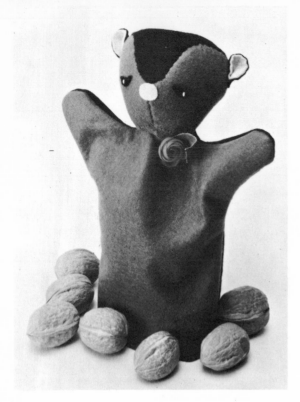

Montgomery Mole

and clip the seam, and turn on to the right side.

With the right sides together, join the two head pieces between the nose and the neck. Now place the pointed tip of the gusset to the top of this seam, right sides together, and join carefully round each side of the head. Clip the seams and turn on to the right side.

Stuff the head firmly and then, with the index finger inside the body, push up into the head and join neatly round the neck, matching the centre front of the neck to the centre front of the body.

To make each ear, join a black and a pink piece with tiny stab stitches round the outside. Now fold as indicated by the broken line on the pattern, with the pink inside, and stitch to the side of the head, following the illustration carefully.

Cut the nose in pink felt and the eyes in black (Fig. 7): embroider tiny pupils in white as indicated on the diagram, and then stick the features into position as illustrated.

Stitch the rosebud under his chin as shown, to make him look lively.

DOMINIC DORMOUSE

Materials:

2 12in. squares of beigey-brown felt
Scraps of black and pink felt
Kapok for stuffing
White embroidery cotton
2 pipe-cleaners
6in. length decorative braid or ribbon
Copydex adhesive

Method: Cut the basic body (Fig. 3) twice, the head twice, the gusset once and the ear twice, all in brown. Then cut the ear twice more in pink (Fig. 8).

With the right sides together, join the two body pieces, leaving the lower edge open. Trim and clip the seam, and turn on to the right side.

With the right sides together, join the two head pieces between the nose and the neck. Now place the pointed tip of the gusset to the top of this seam, right sides together, and join carefully round each side of the head. Clip the

Dominic Dormouse

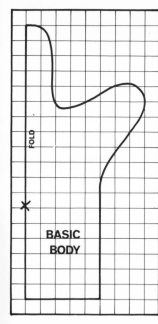

Fig 3. *Oakapple Wood Puppets: basic body. One square=½in.*

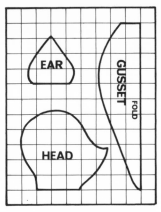

Fig 4. *Cyril Squirrel: head, ear and gusset. One square=½in.*

SQUIRREL

Fig 5. *Cyril Squirrel: eye and nose (to trace)*

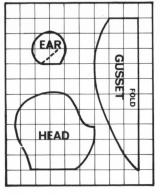

Fig 6. *Montgomery Mole: head ear and gusset. One square=½in.*

MOLE

Fig 7. *Montgomery Mole: eye and nose (to trace)*

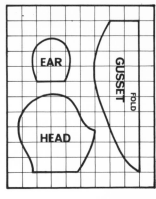

Fig 8. *Dominic Dormouse: head, ear and gusset. One square =½in.*

DORMOUSE

Fig 9. *Dominic Dormouse: eye and nose (to trace)*

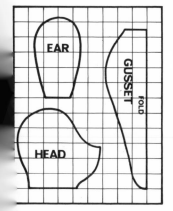

Fig 10. *Rabbit Twins: head, ear and gusset. One square=½in.*

RABBITS

Fig 11. *Rabbit Twins: eye and nose (to trace)*

OWL

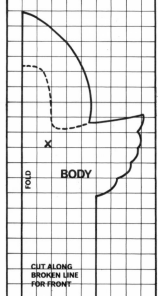

Fig 12. *Mr. Woo, the Owl: body. One square=½in.*

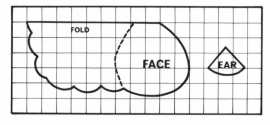

Fig 13. *Mr. Woo, the Owl: face and ear. One square=½in.*

seams and turn on to the right side.

Stuff the head firmly and then, with the index finger inside the body, push up into the head and join neatly round the neck, matching the centre front of the neck to the centre front of the body.

To make each ear, join a brown and a pink piece with tiny stab stitches round the outside. Then stitch to the head, following the illustration carefully.

Cut the nose in pink felt and the eyes in black (Fig. 9): embroider tiny pupils in white as indicated on the diagram, and then stick the features into position as illustrated.

To make his tail, cut a strip of felt 8in. by 2in. and roll it tightly lengthways, with the pipe-cleaners in the centre. Trim one end to

Fig 14. *Mr. Woo, the Owl: eye and beak (to trace)*

11

make a rounded tip, and then slip-stitch the edge of the felt neatly down the length of the tail. Make a slit in the back of the body at point X and push the base of the tail through for about 1in., stitching it firmly to the inside so that the tail stands up straight.

Make the braid or ribbon into a jaunty bow, as shown, and stitch to the centre of his neck

THE RABBIT TWINS

Materials: (for each rabbit)

12in. square of grey felt
12in. square of white felt
Piece of pale pink felt 3in. by 4in.
Scraps of blue or green and black felt
Scrap of lambswool or a pompon of white wool
Kapok for stuffing
Tiny artificial flowers for Moppet
½yd. 1in.-wide woven braid for Hoppit
Copydex adhesive

Method: Cut the basic body (Fig. 3) once each in grey and white, the gusset once and the ear twice in grey, the head twice in white, and the ear twice more in pink (Fig. 10).

With the right sides together, join the two body pieces, leaving the lower edge open. Trim and clip the seam, and turn on to the right side.

With the right sides together, join the two head pieces between the nose and the neck. Now place the rounded tip of the gusset to the top of this seam, right sides together, and join carefully round each side of the head. Clip the seams and turn on to the right side.

Stuff the head firmly and then, with the index finger inside the body, push up into the head and join neatly round the neck, matching the centre front of the neck to the centre front of the body.

To make each ear, join a grey and a pink piece with tiny stab stitches round the outside. Then stitch to the back of the head, following

Moppet Rabbit

Hoppit Rabbit

12

the illustration carefully.

Cut the nose in pink felt, and the eyes in green or blue, with tiny pupils in black (Fig. 11). Stick the features into position as illustrated.

Stitch the lambswool or pompon to the back of the body at point X, for the tail.

Make a pretty necklace of flowers for Moppet, as shown, and a braid muffler for Hoppit (as you did for Cyril).

MR WOO

Materials:

Piece of dark brown felt 10in. by 18in.
6in. square of white felt
Scraps of orange, gold, lemon and black felt
Kapok for stuffing
Copydex adhesive

Method: Cut the body back and front once each in brown as Fig. 12 (note broken line indicating cutting line for the front), the face once in white and the ear four times in brown (Fig. 13).

With the *wrong* sides together, join the body front to the back, leaving the lower edge open. Catch the front and back together at each point X. Trim the edges neatly.

Then, with the *right* sides together, stitch the face to the back of the head between the top of the wings, matching centres. Trim and clip the seam and turn on to the right side. Now stitch the face to the body front as indicated by the broken line, inserting stuffing into the head at each side as you go. Leave the lower part of the face free, to form his chest.

To make each ear, stitch two pieces together round the outside, curve round slightly and stitch to the top of the head as illustrated.

Cut the beak twice in orange felt, the outer eyes in gold, the inner in lemon, and the pupils in black (Fig. 14). Stitch the two beak pieces together, inserting a little stuffing. Then stitch the top edge to the face, just above the centre

Mr. Woo

point of the previous stitching line. Finally, stick the eyes into position as illustrated.

PUPPET THEATRE

Materials:

3 1in. by 1in. battens 18in. long (A)
4 1in. by 1in. battens 16in. long (B)
2 1in. by 1in. battens 13in. long (C)
2 1in. by 1in. battens 8in. long (D)
2 1½in. wide by ¼in. thick strips 18in. long (E)
1 piece of plywood 18½in. by 4in. (F)
1 piece of plywood 18½in. by 4½in. (G)
2 pieces of plywood 5½in. by 4in. (H)
Screws; glue; sandpaper
¼yd. of 36in.-wide green towelling (any rough

13

fabric or felt would be suitable)
Fabric adhesive
Piece of thick card 22in. by 16in. and wallpaper
    to cover
Paste
1½yd. silk braid or similar edging

To make: Cut the 1in. by 1in. battens to
length as above, and pencil the appropriate
letter of the alphabet on each for easy identi-
fication. Now glue and screw together as
shown in Fig. 15, making up the two sides
first and then joining with strips A and E.
Position one strip A across the front to support
the stage, making the *top* edge 3in. up from
vertical side strip B at each side. The distance
between the two strips E at the back should be
6in. (this is important later!).

Now cut and fix the pieces of plywood to
the frame to form the front platform, positioning as shown in Fig. 16. Smooth all over with
sandpaper.

Using fabric adhesive, cover the front platform with towelling to look like grass, folding
the sides neatly and sticking all raw edges
underneath so that they are hidden.

Now cut the card as shown in Fig. 17, and
cover one side with wallpaper, cutting and
folding the corners carefully, and sticking
excess to back round the outside, but leaving
free a 2in. overlap all round the inner edge.
Then glue the card firmly to the front framework above the platform, positioning as
illustrated, and stick the excess wallpaper
neatly round the battens inside.

Finish off by sticking braid round the
outer edge of front.

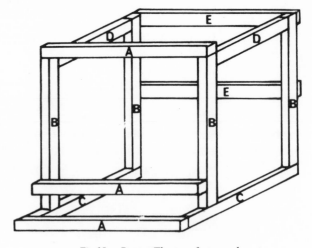

Fig 15.   Puppet Theatre: framework

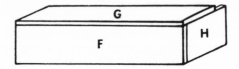

Fig 16.   Puppet Theatre: front platforms

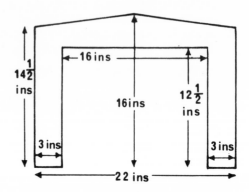

Fig 17.   Puppet Theatre: front frame

Stuff and Nonsense: developing your characters

Stuff and Nonsense

The puppy and kitten you see playing in the photographs are basically no different from the puppets of Oakapple Wood. *That* design has simply been *developed* . . . to give them feet, paws that curve round towards the front of the body, and some simple clothes. But see how these small additions emphasize the characters of the two little animals.

Stuff has a tie and school cap–neither of which he seems capable of wearing at a tidy angle! And Nonsense, has a homely little flowered smock, with a Red Riding Hood cape for when she goes out–which makes her look very capable and domesticated.

Just as with the Oakapple Wood puppets, the features, and their careful positioning, do a great deal to convey the character of each little animal. Notice this especially with Stuff, the puppy, whose eyes are no more than black felt circles: yet placed close to his nose, as in

15

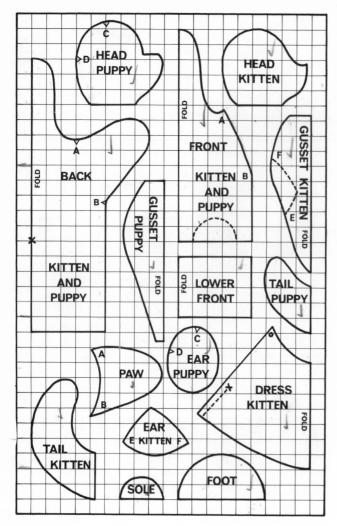

PUPPY

Fig 19. *Stuff (dog): nose and eye (to trace)*

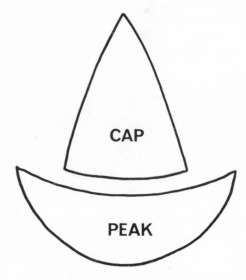

Fig 20. *Stuff (dog): cap (to trace)*

KITTEN

Fig 21. *Nonsense (cat): nose and eye (to trace)*

Fig 18. *Stuff (dog) and Nonsense (cat): patterns.*
One square = $\frac{1}{2}$in.

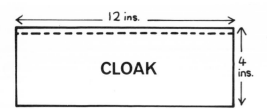

CLOAK

Fig 22. *Nonsense (cat): cloak*

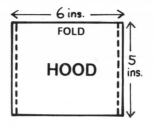

HOOD

Fig 23. *Nonsense (cat): hood*

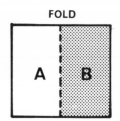

Fig 24. *Nonsense (cat): hood, showing how to fold*

the illustrations, they give him a mischievously intent and very puppy-like expression. But Nonsense's wide blue eyes and little pink nose emphasize her charm and innocence.

You can see just a few of the things Stuff and Nonsense enjoy doing from the pictures. These should give you some ideas to write a play of your own for Stuff and Nonsense to act.

To make your patterns: First rule a sheet of paper into **half-inch squares**—or use graph paper. Then draw out your patterns (Fig. 18). Mark notches and broken lines.

Trace the features, and patterns for Stuff's cap, from the separate diagrams (Figs. 19 and 20).

Make ¼in. seams, unless otherwise directed.

STUFF

Materials:

12in. square of brown felt
9in. square of gold felt
2in. square of pink felt
Scrap of black felt
6in. square of green felt for his cap and tie
Kapok for stuffing
Black embroidery cotton
Thin card
Copydex adhesive

Method: Cut the back, lower front and gusset once each, and the ear, tail and foot twice each, in brown. Cut the front once, and the head, paw and ear twice each in gold. Cut the sole twice in pink.

*With the right sides together, stitch the two paw pieces to the front between points A and B. Stitch the straight edge of each foot to the front, as indicated by the broken line: gather the curved edge. Draw up these gathers to fit round the curved edge of the sole, and oversew on the right side, matching centres and distributing the gathers evenly. Stuff each foot, then pin the straight edge of the sole to

Stuff and Nonsense go sailing

the edge of the front. With right sides together, join the top edge of the lower front to the lower edge of the main front, including the straight edges of the soles as you stitch.

With right sides together, join the back and front, leaving the lower edges open. Trim and clip the seam and turn to the right side.

With the right sides together, join the head pieces between the nose and the neck. Now place the narrow end of the gusset to the top of this seam, right sides together, and join very carefully and evenly round each side of the head. Clip the seams and turn to the right side. Stuff the head firmly, then, with the index finger inside the body, push up into the head and join neatly round the neck, matching centre fronts.

With the right sides together, stitch the tail pieces together round the curved edge. Clip the seam, then turn to the right side and stuff firmly. Stitch to the back of the body at point X.

Embroider three black straight stitches on each paw, as illustrated.*

To make each ear, join a brown and a gold piece, right sides together, all round the curved

17

edge between points C and D. Turn to the right side. Cut two or three 1¼in. diameter circles of felt, and insert in the base of each ear. Stitch firmly to each side of his head, matching the notches.

Cut the nose once and the eye twice in black felt (Fig. 19). Stick into position as illustrated.

Stuff's tie: Cut two ½in.-wide strips of green felt and join them together to form one long strip.

Cap: Cut the cap section of the pattern seven times, and the peak twice. With the right sides together, stitch sections together to form a circle, with all the points meeting at the centre. Cut the peak again in thin card, and stick between the two felt pieces. Stitch the inner curve of the peak to the edge of the cap, and embroider his initial on the front.

NONSENSE

Materials:

12in. square of grey felt
9in. square of white felt
Piece of pink felt 3in. by 4in.
Scraps of blue and black felt
Kapok for stuffing
Black embroidery cotton
Piece of fabric 10in. by 8in. for her dress
Bias binding to trim
2 press fasteners
Piece of fabric 12in. by 10in. for her cloak
½yd. matching narrow ribbon
Copydex adhesive

Method: Cut the back, lower front and gusset once each, and the ear, paw, tail and foot twice each, in grey. Cut the front once, and the head twice, in white. Cut the ear and the sole twice each in pink.

Now follow the instructions for making Stuff from * to *.

More Stuff and Nonsense

To make each ear, join a grey and a pink piece, right sides together, leaving the curved edge open between points E and F. Turn to the right side and stitch firmly to the head as indicated by the broken line on the gusset.

Cut the nose in pink felt and the eye twice in blue, with black pupils (Fig. 21). Stick into position as illustrated.

To make her dress, cut the pattern piece twice in fabric. Then, with right sides together, join the two pieces, stitching along the broken line below X to form the side seams. Hem the raw edges at each side above X to make the armholes. Bind the neck edges and then stitch a press fastener at each point O to fasten at the sides of the neck. Hem the lower edge neatly.

Cut the pieces for her cloak and hood as shown in Figs. 22 and 23.

Gather the top edge of the cloak as indicated on Fig. 22, and narrowly hem the other edges. With the hood still folded as in Fig. 23, stitch each side as indicated, then turn to the right side so that it looks like Fig. 24: now push the shaded half–B–inside A. The broken line now forms the front edge of the hood.

Draw up the cloak gathers to fit, and stitch to the lower edge of the hood, with the gathers between the turned up inside and outside edges.

Halve the ribbon and stitch a tie at each side of the neck.

Lord and Lady Horseshoe: human characterization

Our final pair of glove puppets is a man and a woman. If you look at the people around you in a bus or train–or anywhere else, for that matter–you will realize just how different they all are. And then it is interesting to decide *why* each is so different from his or her neighbour– what it is you most notice about him or her– what makes a particular person distinctive. Some people seem to fade into the background and you scarcely notice them, whilst others are instantly recognizable if you meet them again. They might have a droopy moustache– or a neatly clipped one–a beard, heavy spectacles, a flowery hat, an old-fashioned hairstyle, rows and rows of coloured beads, check trousers, funny shoes, a tightly-rolled umbrella . . .

Take Lord and Lady Horseshoe, for instance. Did you ever see a more aristocratic looking elderly couple? Lady Horseshoe has her grey hair neatly piled on top of her head in a bun, she wears small gold-rimmed spectacles, and has a gentle, slightly prim, expression: her high-necked, flowered dress is rather old-fashioned–and her earrings are obviously family heirlooms! Her husband's rather florid complexion and large nose are the result of a life-long fondness for whisky, but his monocle and fierce moustache indicate that he is a stern disciplinarian! His stiff white collar, fancy tie and side-whiskers all show that he takes a pride in his appearance.

Notice their eyes. Both have small round buttons with two holes. But whilst Lady Horseshoe's bright blue ones are sewn on with a vertical line of black cotton to give her an alert expression, her husband's slightly bleary look is achieved with white cotton stitched horizontally across the buttons. And their hair. Both use ordinary knitting wool: Lady Horseshoe's straight grey hair is plain double-knitting (if you are using a finer ply, simply use more wool), but Lord Horseshoe's crinkly hair and military moustache are an unevenly textured yarn. You can have great fun examining the wide range of novelty knitting wools available now, and visualizing them as hairstyles for your puppets and soft toys.

To make your patterns: First rule a sheet of paper into **half-inch squares**–or use graph paper. Then draw out your patterns following Fig. 25. Mark notches, darts, etc., and broken lines.

Trace Lady Horseshoe's mouth from Fig. 26.

Make ¼in. seams, unless otherwise directed.

LORD HORSESHOE

Materials:

Rose pink felt 6in. by 9in.
White felt 10in. by 8in.
Mid-green felt 6in. by 5in. for his trousers
Dark-green felt 9in. by 8in. for his jacket
Grey felt 2in. by 5in.
Scrap of brown felt and a 3in. diameter circle
1½in. diameter circle of black felt
Kapok for stuffing
5in. length 1in.-wide stiff white ribbon for collar
Scrap of patterned fabric or ribbon about 3in. by 1in.
Beige wool or yarn for hair (illustrated is Twilley's Bubbly)
3 tiny brown buttons for jacket
2 tiny black "fish-eye" buttons for eyes
1in. diameter brass curtain ring
5in. length of tiny gold beads, fine chain, fine gold cord or gift-tie string, for monocle
Copydex adhesive

Method: Cut the head back and front and the

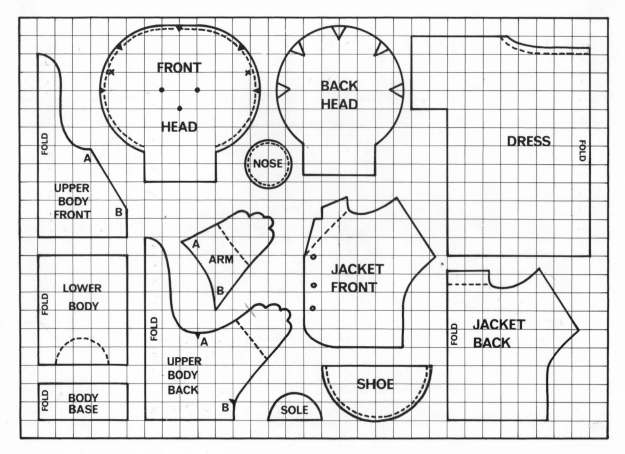

Fig 25. *Lord and Lady Horseshoe: patterns. One square = ½ in.*

MOUTH

Fig 26. Lady Horseshoe: mouth (to trace)

nose once each, and the hand four times, in pink felt (cut the hand from the arm pattern piece, ending at the broken line). Cut the upper body back and front once each in white, and the arm twice, omitting the hand beyond the broken line on back and arm: cut the lower body twice in mid-green, the base twice in grey, the shoe twice in brown and the sole twice in black.

With the right sides together, stitch the two arm pieces to the upper body front between points A and B: then stitch a hand to the end

of each arm on the back and front (thumbs up).

*With the right sides together, stitch the lower edge of each upper body piece to the top edge of a lower body piece. Stitch the straight edge of each shoe to the body front, as indicated by the broken line: then gather the curved edge. Draw up gathers to fit round the curved edge of the sole, and oversew on the right side, matching centres and distributing the gathers evenly. Stuff each foot, then pin the straight edge of the sole to the edge of the body front. With right sides together, join the top edge of the base to the lower edge of the front, including the straight edges of the soles as you stitch. Join the second base piece to the lower edge of the back. Press. With right sides together, join the back and front (oversew the hands, to emphasize finger detail), leaving the

lower edges open. Trim and clip the seam, then turn to the right side.

On the wrong side of the fabric, pin and stitch the darts round the back of the head, and run a gathering thread round the front, as indicated on the pattern. Run a gathering thread round the outer edge of the nose: place a tiny piece of stuffing in the centre, and then draw up the thread as tightly as possible. Pin to the centre of the front head, as indicated on the pattern, and stitch firmly into position from the wrong side of the head. With right sides together, pin the darts to correspond with the notches, draw up thread to fit, distributing gathers evenly. Join the front head to the back round the outer edge, leaving the lower edge open. Clip curves and turn to the right side. Stuff firmly. Then, with the index finger inside the body, push up into the head and join neatly round the neck, matching sides and centres.*

To make his moustache, cut a piece of card 4in. deep by about 2in. wide. Wind the yarn right round the card about twenty times (according to thickness): slip carefully off the card and tie tightly at the centre. Stitch to the face close under the nose, as illustrated.

Make the hair in the same way, but begin with his side-whiskers by winding the yarn ten times round a 1in. deep piece of card for each: cut one looped end, and stitch the other to the side of the face at X. Then wind the yarn about twenty times round a 5½in. deep card: slip off card and tie tightly at the centre, stitching this to the top point of the head, over the seam. Catch the looped ends to the side of the face, just in front of the seam, at each side. Wind the yarn about thirty times round a 6in. deep card: tie loosely at the centre and stitch to the top of the head, behind the first piece. Catch the looped ends at each side, over the seam. Finally, wind the yarn about forty times round a 5in. deep card: tie tightly at the centre and then stitch to the crown of the head, behind the previous piece. Spread the looped ends out to cover the back of the head, and catch neatly into place. Trim side-whiskers neatly.

Cut two ⅝in. diameter circles of brown felt for the eyes: stitch a black "fish-eye" button in the centre of each, using white thread. Stick the back of the felt to the face, slightly wider apart than the positions indicated on the pattern: the white stitching line horizontal, as illustrated.

Fold back the cut ends of the white ribbon, and stitch the lower edge round the neck, as shown. Fold the "tie" of patterned fabric into a strip ⅜in. wide, and stitch one end to the neck, behind the collar, bringing it over and down as illustrated, catching with long horizontal stitches level with the lower edge of the collar, to resemble a knot, and then catching the lower end to the body.

To make his jacket, cut the back once and the front twice, in dark green felt (Fig. 25). With the right sides together, join the fronts to the back along the shoulder, sleeve and side seams (turning to stitch the collar on the *right* side beyond the broken line). Clip the seams and curves, turn to the right side, and fold the collar down as indicated by the broken lines on the pattern. Fit on to puppet: pin the centre fronts together and stitch a button at each point O on the pattern, through both thicknesses of felt.

Stitch the curtain ring firmly at the side of the nose, positioned over one eye, as illustrated. Catch at the other side and then attach a length of chain, or beads, or cord, etc: catch the other end behind his lapel.

LADY HORSESHOE

Materials:

Flesh pink felt 9in. by 15in.
White felt 6in. by 5in.
Grey felt 4in. by 6in.
1½in. diameter circle of black felt
Scrap of bright pink felt for her mouth
Kapok for stuffing
Piece of fabric 12in. by 10in. for her dress
5in. ⅝in.-wide ribbon for collar

22

$\frac{3}{8}$yd. narrow trimming (lace, etc.)
$\frac{1}{2}$yd. 1in.-wide lace to trim "petticoat"
Mid-grey double knitting wool for hair
2 tiny blue "fish-eye" buttons for eyes
2 $\frac{5}{8}$in. diameter brass curtain rings for
    spectacles
Matching gold embroidery cotton for
    spectacles
2 large and 2 tiny beads for earrings
Copydex adhesive

Method: Cut the head back and front, and the upper body back and front, once each, and the arm twice, in pink felt. Cut the lower body twice in white, the base and shoe twice each in grey, and the sole twice in black.

With the right sides together, stitch the two arm pieces to the upper body front between points A and B. Now follow the instructions for making Lord Horseshoe between * and *, *but ignore directions for nose.*

To make her hair, cut a piece of card 7in. deep by about 2in. wide. Wind the wool right round the card about twenty times (according to thickness). Pass a thread of wool through the loops at each end, and tie loosely: slip carefully off the card and tie tightly at the centre. Stitch to the top point of the head, just in front of the seam: catch the loops over the seam at each side. Now wind the wool about twenty times round a 5$\frac{1}{2}$in. deep card: tie the loops very loosely, and then the centre tightly, as before. Stitch to the top of the head behind the first piece, and spread the looped ends out to cover the back of the head, catching neatly into place. Finally, wind the wool loosely round two fingers, about fifty times, for her bun. Catch the loops together lightly, to prevent unravelling, and stitch to the top of her head, as illustrated.

Stitch the buttons to her face with black thread, slightly closer together than the positions indicated on the pattern, the stitching line vertical, as illustrated. Stitch the curtain rings over her eyes, catching to the face at each side, and join with a buttonhole-stitched bar across the centre.

Cut the mouth (Fig. 26) in bright pink felt and stick into position as illustrated.

Stitch a large bead to each side of the face, as shown, anchoring each with a tiny bead underneath, so that the earrings will hang freely.

Gather the lace and stitch round white edge of lower body, near the base, to trim her "petticoat".

To make her dress (Fig. 25), cut the pattern twice in fabric. With the right sides together, join the shoulder, sleeve and side seams. Turn up a $\frac{1}{4}$in. hem round the sleeves. Trim and clip the seams, turn to the right side, and run a gathering thread round the neck, as indicated. Fit on to puppet and draw up gathers to fit round neck: then stitch one side of the ribbon over the raw gathered edge, turning the cut ends under and joining the collar at the back of the neck. Stitch trimming round sleeves and top of collar, and turn up hem, as shown.

The Eskimoes of Igloo Island: finger puppets

Now let's try some smaller, quick-to-make, puppets. Each one fits over one finger only– so although you can't animate them like glove puppets, you can have up to five characters on one hand! And because of the way they are made–using bouncy foam–you'll be surprised how much animation you can achieve just by jogging them about on your hand.

We'll begin with a family of Eskimoes. Dressed in traditional costume, with great shaggy fur-edged hoods, their special clothes and national characteristics in appearance make it particularly easy to convey identity.

You can buy foam sheeting in Woolworth's –or it is stocked by most hardware stores and many chemists (large pieces are often used as bath sheets). If you can't find it quite as thin as stated, a slightly thicker sheet won't matter (or you *could* even cut slices from an inexpensive foam sponge).

Instructions are given for making the basic figure, followed by individual variations for each character.

To make your patterns: The diagrams are all actual size, so you need only to trace them.

THE BASIC FIGURE

Materials:

Thin sheet foam (about $\frac{1}{8}$in. thick)
1 table-tennis ball
1 pipe-cleaner
Flesh-coloured felt
Coloured felt to dress
Dark brown double knitting wool
White wool fringe about 1in. deep–or cotton wool
Narrow embroidered ribbon to trim
2 small round buttons or beads (about $\frac{3}{8}$in. diameter)

3 tiny beads (for child)
Flesh-coloured poster paint
Black paint or ink
Evo-stik clear adhesive

Method:

For the adults: Cut a piece of foam 4in. by $2\frac{1}{2}$in., as Fig. 27: cut two $\frac{1}{2}$in.-long slits equidistant from the centre, as indicated. Fold over and join the sides to form a centre back seam (oversew the foam).

Cut a $2\frac{1}{2}$in. by $\frac{1}{2}$in. strip of foam for the arms, a $2\frac{3}{4}$in. length of pipe-cleaner, and the longer arm pattern in felt (Fig. 28). Place the pipe-cleaner on the foam, slightly overlapping each end. Fold the foam round the cleaner, and catch the edges together to hold in place. Place the padded pipe-cleaner on the felt, hands extending beyond the cleaner at each end, fold the felt round, and oversew the edges together between the wrists, leaving the hands open.

Your basic figure is now ready to be dressed. Cut a piece of felt 3in. wide by 2in. deep for the trousers. Fold over and join the short edges to form the centre front seam. Turn to the right side and fit over the foam figure, the lower edges of the foam and felt level: catch the top edge to the foam. Stitch buttons or beads at the lower edge for the feet, as illustrated.

Cut the adult anorak in felt (Fig. 29). Fold over as indicated by the broken line and join the side and sleeve seams. Turn to the right side. Stick ribbon round sleeves, lower edge, and down the front, as illustrated. Fit the anorak on the figure, at the same time pushing the arms through the slits in the body (thumbs up).

Now fix the head. Make a small hole in the table-tennis ball with the point of your scissors, then carefully push the foam at the top of the figure (above the broken line) inside

24

the ball, so that it is held firmly in position. Paint the ball with flesh-coloured poster paint and add hair, hoods, etc., as the individual instructions below. Then draw the features in black, following the illustration.

Father: Cut a 4½in. diameter semi-circle of felt for his hood. Gather the straight, lower edge and draw up to fit round his neck. Gather all round the curved edge, and draw up to fit loosely round the face. Fold a 12in. length of fringe in half, and stitch the top edges of this double thickness round the inside of the curved edge, positioning the gathers mainly at the centre. If you are using cotton wool, stick it round the outside edge of the hood.

Wind dark brown wool about 15 times round a 1½in. deep piece of card. Tie the loops together tightly and slip off the card. Stitch inside the front of the hood, protruding as illustrated. Fit the hood on his head, catch the corners together under his chin, and the back edge to the top of his anorak. Fluff out the fringe, as shown.

Grandpa: Make his hood as for Father—but don't give him any hair, because he's bald! When the hood is fixed on his head, make his beard by winding grey double-knitting wool 10 times round a 1½in. deep piece of card. Tie the loops together tightly at one side, then cut them at the other. Stick to the lower part of his face, as illustrated.

Mother and baby: Cut a piece of felt 1½in. wide by 1in. deep, and slip-stitch to the back of her anorak, the lower edges level, leaving the top open to form a pocket. Fix double fringe round her neck and then trim it shorter as illustrated.

Wind brown wool 20 times round a 5in. deep piece of card. Tie the loops at each side, then slide off the card and tie loosely round the centre. Stick the centre to the top of the head, then take the loops round to the back as illustrated, sticking at each side, so that they meet at the back of her neck: tie the loops

together neatly.

Use a round button or wooden ball for the baby's head—or make it from Plasticine or Harbutt's self-hardening Plastone, painting it if necessary. Push a matchstick into the head. Wrap some foam round the matchstick, then cover it with felt. Stick a little cotton wool round the neck. Wind brown wool 10 times round a 1½in. deep piece of card. Slide carefully off the card, tie tightly round the centre and then cut the loops at each side. Stick to the top of the baby's head and trim, as illustrated.

Add the features as shown in the picture and fit inside the pocket at the back of mother's anorak.

For the children: Make the body as instructed for the adults, but cut the foam only 3in. by 2½in., as indicated on Fig. 27.

Make the arms as for the adult, but cut your foam only 1½in. by ½in., a 1¾in. length of pipe-cleaner, and use the shorter arm pattern, cutting the hands a little smaller.

Your basic figure is now ready to be dressed. Cut the anorak in felt (Fig. 30). Fold over as indicated by the broken line, then join the side and sleeve seams. Turn the lower half *only* to the right side, and stick trimming round the edge, with the join at the centre front. Then turn back to the wrong side, fold down the centre front and oversew the folded edge below X to form a tuck for the leg division. Turn to the right side, stick trimming round sleeves, and sew three tiny beads down the front for buttons. Fit the anorak on the figure, pushing the arms through the slits in the body (thumbs up). Stitch buttons or beads at the lower edge for feet, as shown.

Fix and paint the head as for the adults. Make the hood and front hair as for the adult, but trim the "fur" fringe a little shorter when the hood is in position.

Girl: Wind brown wool 15 times round a 7in. deep piece of card. Tie the loops at each side, then slide off the card and tie loosely round

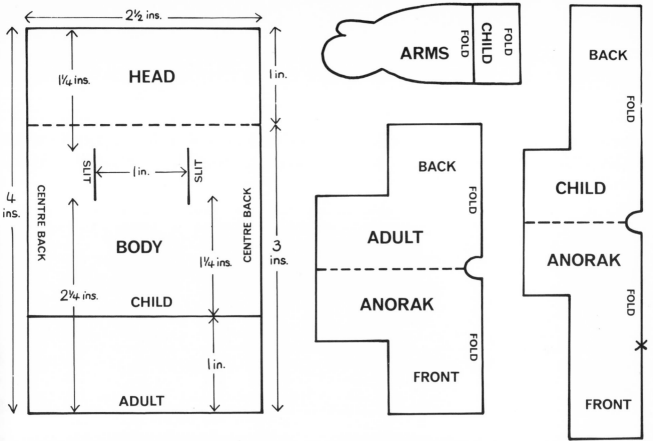

Fig 27.   *Eskimoes: basic body for adult and child (to trace)*

Fig 28.   *Eskimoes: arms for adult and child (to trace)*

Fig 29.   *Eskimoes: adult's anorak (to trace)*

Fig 30.   *Eskimoes: child's anorak (to trace)*

the centre. Stick the centre to the top of her head, then take the loops down, sticking to the sides and back, to neck level. Tie the wool tightly round the remaining section of each loop, and trim the ends to form plaits, as illustrated. Stick cotton wool round her neck.

The three children

27

All Kinds of Finger People: variations on the basic design

Having made the Eskimoes, you'll probably be keen to develop the finger puppet design and create all sorts of different characters. It isn't difficult, as you can see from the picture on the jacket: from Old King Cole to Scruffy the dog–all are based on the same sheet-foam body and table-tennis ball head. And all are perfectly easy to make if you follow the individual instructions and study the picture on the jacket.

These are just to show you how. Soon you'll be creating a whole host of quite different finger people of your own. Remember to study the character you want to create very carefully before you begin, so that you can emphasize the most distinctive features–like Professor Noodle's bald head and droopy moustache, Mrs Dumpling's homely hairstyle or Old King Cole's regal robes . . .

To make your patterns: The easiest way to draw out the patterns from Fig. 31 is to use squared or graph paper: measure the scale of the squares and then draw up the diagrams to the correct size. The remaining patterns are actual size, so need only to be traced.

THE BASIC FIGURE

Materials:

Thin sheet foam (about $\frac{1}{8}$in. thick)
Table-tennis ball
Pipe-cleaner
Flesh-coloured felt
2 small round buttons or beads (about $\frac{1}{2}$in. diameter)
Flesh-coloured poster paint
Black paint or ink
Evo-stik clear adhesive

Method: Cut a piece of foam 3in. by 2½in., as Fig. 31: cut two ½in. long slits equi-distant from the centre, as indicated. Fold over and join the sides to form a centre back seam (oversew the foam).

Cut a 2½in. by ½in. strip of foam for the arms, a 2¾in. length of pipe-cleaner, and the arm pattern in felt (Fig. 32). Place the pipe-cleaner on the foam, slightly overlapping each end. Fold the foam round the cleaner and catch the edges together to hold in place. Place the padded pipe-cleaner on the felt, hands extending beyond cleaner at each end, fold the felt round and oversew the edges together between the wrists, leaving the hands open. Push the arms through the slits in the body (thumbs up).

Cut two pieces of foam 2in. long by 1in. wide, for the legs. Fold each in half lengthways, and join the edges to form a tube. Stitch the top edge of each leg (join at centre back) to the front of the body, side-by-side, about ¼in. above the lower edge (as indicated by the broken lines on Fig. 31).

Your basic figure is now ready to be dressed. Each character is described individually below, and you will find the points at which you should fit the head and add the shoes.

To fix the head: make a small hole in the table-tennis ball with the point of your scissors: then carefully push the foam at the top of the body (above the broken line on the diagram) inside the ball, so that it is held firmly in position. Unless otherwise instructed, paint with flesh-coloured poster paint, and add the features in black as illustrated.

For the shoes: sew the round buttons or beads to the base of each leg, masking the tops with trousers or pantalettes.

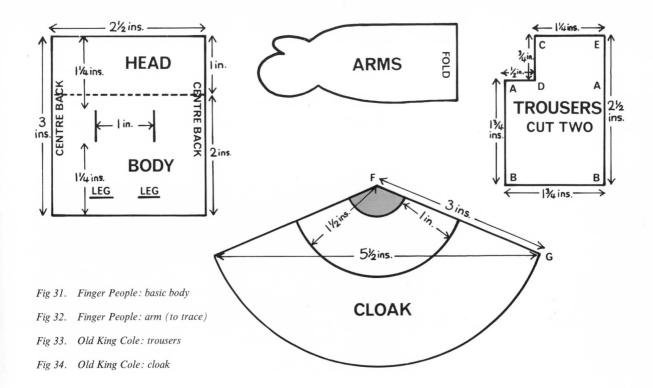

Fig 31.   Finger People: basic body

Fig 32.   Finger People: arm (to trace)

Fig 33.   Old King Cole: trousers

Fig 34.   Old King Cole: cloak

OLD KING COLE

Old King Cole is top left in the picture on the
    jacket.

Materials:

The basic figure
Purple and white felt for his cloak
Lilac felt for his sleeves
Green felt for his trousers
3½in. 1¼in.-wide embroidered ribbon for tunic
½yd. narrow white velvet ribbon
4in. gold braid for crown
Scrap of white lace
Cotton wool
2in. narrow red ribbon
A tiny round wooden button or bead and a
    cocktail stick or matchstick for his pipe
Bowl-shaped small silver button
Copydex adhesive
Evo-stik clear adhesive

Method: Cut two pieces of green felt as Fig. 33
for his trousers. Fold each in half lengthways
and join the side edges between A and B. Turn
both pieces on to the right side. Then, with
right sides together, join the two halves
between C and D. Fit trousers on puppet
figure (lower edges of legs and trousers level),
and join points E together at the back,
catching to the body at back and front.

Cut a piece of lilac felt 3in. by 1½in. for the
sleeves. Make a ¼in. lengthways slit in the
centre, then fold in half lengthways and join
the edges for 1in. from each end leaving 1in.
open at the centre. Turn and fit on figure.
Stick white velvet ribbon round cuffs, as
illustrated, and mark "ermine" with black ink.

Turn under and hem the cut ends of the
ribbon for the tunic. Fold in half, hemmed
edges together, and make a ¼in. slit along the
fold. Fit on the figure and catch side edges of
back and front together under each arm.

Make a paper pattern for his cloak by
drawing a 3in. radius semi-circle. Draw a

straight line from the centre to the outer edge (F-G on Fig. 34). Now put the point of your compasses at G, and with a $5\frac{1}{2}$in. radius, mark the edge of the circle (point H). Then join H-F. With centre F again, draw a $\frac{1}{2}$in. radius semi-circle, and then a $1\frac{1}{2}$in. radius semi-circle for the cape, as Fig. 34. Cut away the shaded centre section. Cut the complete cloak in purple felt, and the cape only in white. Stick folded velvet ribbon down the front edges of the cloak, and flat round the lower edge. Stick the cape on top. Mark "ermine" as before. Fit on the figure and catch top corners together at the neck, covering with a scrap of gathered white lace to form a cravat.

Fit orange shoes as instructed on page 28, and trim tops with a 1in. length of red ribbon caught at the centre to form a bow.

Fix and paint the head as instructed on page 28, and stick cotton wool round as illustrated (using clear adhesive) for hair and beard. Join the cut ends of the gold braid and stick crown in position. Paint his eyes and a pink nose. Push the stick through the wooden button or ball and stick firmly. Trim protruding end, and cut stem of pipe 1in. long. Make a hole in the ball, through the beard, and push the pipe through.

Stitch bowl-shaped button to hand, as shown.

MRS DUMPLING

Mrs Dumpling is top right in the picture on the jacket.

Materials:

The basic figure
Blue cotton fabric for her dress
6in. 3in.-deep lace for petticoat
4in. 1in.-deep broderie anglaise
Grey knitting wool
Tiny coloured glass beads for necklace

Method: Cut 2in. lengths of broderie anglaise — one for each leg. Fold in half, right side inside, and join the cut edges. Then turn each to the right side to form a tube and stitch round each leg, lower edges of pantalettes and legs level.

With the right side inside, join the cut edges of the lace. Turn to right side, gather top edge, and draw up to measure 3in. Fit on the figure, join at the back, and catch to the foam $\frac{1}{4}$in. below arms.

Cut a piece of fabric for the skirt 3in. deep by 9in. wide. Make up the skirt and fit on the figure as described for the petticoat, turning up a hem round the lower edge, and catching the top edge to the foam just above the lace. Cut the sleeves $2\frac{1}{2}$in. deep by $3\frac{1}{2}$in. wide. Fold in half lengthways, right side inside, and make a $\frac{1}{2}$in. slit along fold at centre. Join lower edges for $1\frac{1}{4}$in. from each end, leaving 1in. open at the centre. Turn to the right side and fit on the figure. Turn edges of lower centre opening under, and slip-stitch over gathers of skirt. Turn the wrist edges under and gather to fit.

Fit blue shoes: fix and paint the head as previously instructed. For her hair, wind grey wool round a 4in. piece of card (the number of times will depend on the thickness of your wool – double knitting would be 20 times). Slide carefully off the card and tie loosely at the centre. Stick the centre to the top of the head (using clear adhesive), bringing the loops down at each side and sticking into place to cover the sides and back of the head as illustrated. For her bun, wind the wool tightly round the tip of your finger the same number of times as before. Slip a length of wool through the centre and tie tightly. Trim the ends and stick to the top of the head.

Paint her eyes, nose and mouth, following the illustration carefully, and tie beads round her neck as shown.

LUCY ELLEN

Lucy Ellen is between Old King Cole and Mrs Dumpling on the jacket.

Materials:

The basic figure
Flowered cotton for her skirt
Check gingham for her petticoat
Lace for her blouse
5in. 1½in.-deep broderie anglaise
4in. narrow lace
4in. narrow green ribbon
A skein of brown soft embroidery cotton for
  her hair (or use wool)

Method: Cut the broderie anglaise into two 2½in. lengths and follow the directions for making Mrs Dumpling's pantalettes.

Make up the check gingham as Mrs Dumpling's skirt, and catch to the body ¼in. below the arms. Then make up the flowered fabric in the same way, and catch the top edge to the body close under the arms.

Cut a piece of lace 4in. by 2½in. for the sleeves, and make up as for Mrs Dumpling, catching to the top of the skirt in the same way. Tie the ribbon round her waist and knot at the back.

Fit green shoes, and fix and paint her head, following instructions for basic figure.

Gather the narrow lace round her neck, as illustrated.

For her hair, take the skein of embroidery cotton (or wind wool round a 6in. deep card, as for Mrs Dumpling) and tie loosely at the centre. Stick the centre to the top of her head, bringing the loops down at each side, and sticking into place to cover the sides and back of the head (using clear adhesive), as illustrated.

Paint her eyes, nose and mouth, as shown.

PROFESSOR NOODLE

He is the puppet on the bottom right of the picture.

Materials:

The basic figure

Dark green felt for his trousers
Light green felt for waistcoat
Light brown felt for jacket
4in. ⅜in.-wide embroidered ribbon
3 tiny gilt beads
Wool and narrow ribbon or tape for his hair

Method: Cut, make and fit trousers as for Old King Cole.

Fit brown shoes (those in the picture are wooden buttons), and fix and paint his head, following instructions for basic figure.

Trace pattern for waistcoat (Fig. 35) and cut in light green felt. Stitch the beads at the points indicated, for buttons, then stitch the waistcoat to the figure's shoulder at each side, and catch to the top of his trousers behind the lowest button.

Trace pattern for jacket (Fig. 36) and cut in light brown felt. Open out the felt and fold as indicated by the broken line. Join the side and sleeve seams. Turn to the right side and fit on the figure. Catch the lower corners at sides of waistcoat behind the jacket, to hold in place.

Catch the ribbon together to form an inch-wide bow at the centre, then fix round neck as

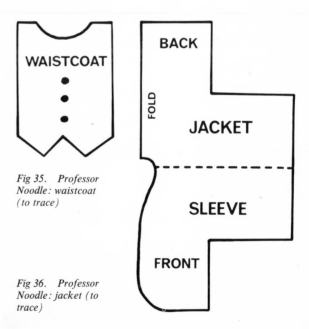

Fig 35. Professor Noodle: waistcoat (to trace)

Fig 36. Professor Noodle: jacket (to trace)

31

shown, joining and trimming the ends at the back.

For his hair, cut a 4in. length of narrow ribbon or tape. Cut a number of 2½in. lengths of wool. Stick these side-by-side along the tape, to cover the middle 3in., the centre of each strand of wool level with the top edge of the tape. Turn the tape to the other side, fold the wool over the top edge and stick to the other side. Fold the ends of the tape in and stick over the wool. Stick this side of the "fringe" to his head (using clear adhesive), as illustrated, and trim neatly to length.

Cut 1in. lengths of wool for his moustache (from 5 to 12, according to thickness). Bind tightly at the centre with cotton, then fold in half and catch together to hold in position. Trim and stick to the face as illustrated.

Paint dots for eyes as shown in the picture.

BABY BUNTING

Follow the directions for the basic figure, but cut the foam, pipe-cleaner and felt each 1in. shorter, make the hands a little smaller, and omit the legs altogether. Baby Bunting is in the extreme left of the picture.

Materials:

The basic figure
Fabric for dress and bonnet
6in. length lace to trim dress
¼yd. ¾in.-wide lace to trim bonnet (or use double this width, folded along the centre – as pictured)
¼yd. narrow white ribbon
Scrap of wool for hair

Method: Cut two pieces of fabric 3½in. wide by 3½in. deep for the dress. With the right sides together, join the side edges to within 1in. from the top: hem remainder at each side to form sleeves. Turn up lower edge and trim with lace, as illustrated. Turn to the right side, then turn top edges under and gather close to

fold. Fit on the figure and draw up tightly at neck level.

Fix and paint the head as instructed.

Cut a 6in. diameter semi-circle for the bonnet. Turn the straight (back) edge under, turn in each end, and gather: draw up to measure 1½in. Turn the front, curved edge under and gather: fit on head and draw up round the face. Stitch gathered lace round front edge, and attach ribbon for ties.

Tie a small knot of wool for her hair, and stick to the head just inside the front of the bonnet.

Paint eyes, nose and mouth, as illustrated.

SCRUFFY

Follow the directions for the basic body, but omit arms and legs. He is at the front in the picture, between Baby Bunting and Lucy Ellen.

Materials:

Basic body and head
1yd. 1in.-deep beige silk lampshade fringe
Matching beige felt
Matching poster paint
Scrap of dark brown felt for ears and paws

Method: Cut a piece of beige felt 2in. deep by 2½in. wide: fold in half and join the shorter sides. Turn to the right side. Gather round the top edge: fit over foam body, seams and lower edges level, then draw gathers up tightly at neck level.

Fix the head as instructed, and paint it to match the body.

Now, beginning at the back, stitch the top edge of the fringe round the lower edge of the felt, continuing round and round the body, each layer of fringe overlapping the one below, until you reach the neck. This time turn the top of the fringe upwards, and stick round base of head (using clear adhesive). Finish off neatly at the back.

Cut his ears in dark brown felt (Fig. 37).

Make another hole, at the top of the head, and stick the ears at each side, overlapping the face as illustrated. Stick a circle of fringe round the hole, flat against the head. Now cut 1½in. of fringe and roll the top edge tightly round like a Swiss roll: stick the end and then push the rolled top edge of the fringe down into the hole. Stick layers of fringe across the back of the head, hiding the cut ends under the ears.

Trace pattern for paws (Fig. 38) and cut in dark brown felt. Stick to front of body as shown. Paint eyes and nose as illustrated.

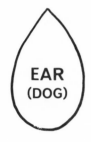

Fig 38. Scruffy (dog): paw (to trace)

Fig 37. Scruffy (dog): ear (to trace)

Jumping Jack and Jill: cardboard puppets to hang on the wall

Here's yet another kind of puppet. This one is simply made from card, with the arms and legs linked together at the back, so that when you pull a central string beneath, the puppet leaps into action and dances a lively jig. Even when they aren't being animated, these happy-go-lucky puppets make an attractive decoration just hanging on the wall of your room.

All you have to do is trace the separate pieces on to stiff card, paint or crayon them in brilliant colours, cut them out and then fix them together with paper fasteners and thread or string as shown.

Materials:

Stiff white card
Small paper fasteners (7 for Jack – 4 for Jill)
Fine string or thick thread
Paints, crayons or felt pens

Method: Trace the separate pieces for each puppet (Figs. 39 and 40) carefully on to fairly stiff white card, making sure you mark the black dots on the different parts (including the one inside the handle of Jack's pail). Paint or crayon in bright colours. Then cut each piece out and make a hole at every point indicated by a black dot (use a punch to do this if you have one): notice that there are *two* holes at the top of each arm and leg, and also one at the top of the head.

Now assemble the puppet by pushing a paper fastener through the hole in the body at each side of the chest, and then through the *lower* hole at the top of each arm (thumbs down). Open out the fasteners at the back so that the arm hangs quite loosely and can move freely – this is important.

Join the top of each of Jack's upper legs under the body in the same way (through the

34

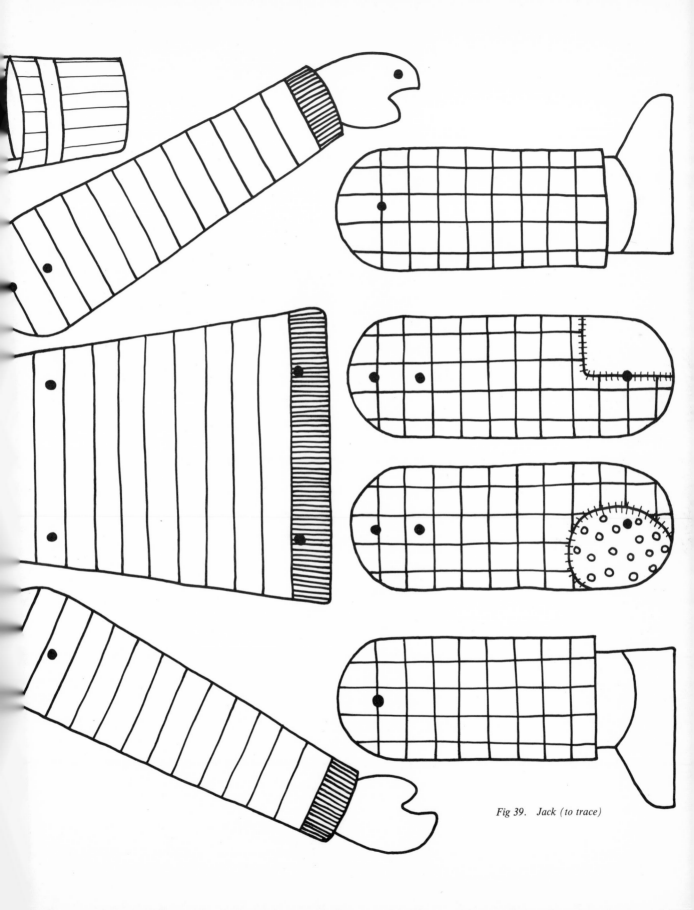

Fig 39. Jack (to trace)

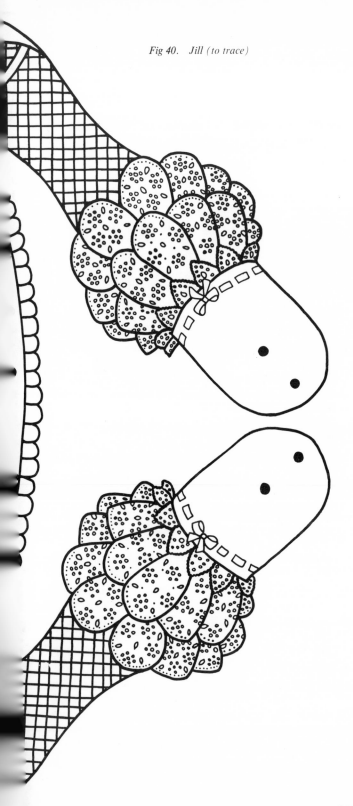

Fig 40.   Jill (to trace)

lower hole again), and then the lower leg behind the upper part, with the knee patches on top. Fix the pail to his hand with another fastener, the hand on top.

For Jill, simply join the top of each leg behind the skirt (through the *lower* hole, as before).

Now turn the figure face down and arrange the arms and legs as positioned in Fig. 39– *all* Jack's limbs *straight down,* but Jill's *arms* slightly raised, as shown. Taking care to keep the limbs in this position, tie the tops of the arms together through the upper holes, as indicated by the broken line in Figs. 39 and 40. Tie the tops of the legs together in the same way.

Now tie one end of a 12in. length of string to the centre of the string joining the arms: then tie it securely round the centre of the leg string, keeping it taut between the two, and allowing the remainder to hang loosely between the puppet's legs.

Turn the puppets over again, fix a loop through the top hole to hang up–and pull the string to make them jump!

The Ragged Scarecrows: a family of marionettes

For our final type of puppet, we're going to look at the kind that are animated by strings – these are called marionettes. They can move their bodies and limbs in the most realistic way, and they can be very simple – with just a few strings – or quite complicated – with a great many strings. These strings are fixed at different points of the body (the joints of which must be very loose), and then attached to a control bar which is held above the puppet. To make the body or limbs move you simply pull the appropriate string. Simple marionettes are easy to work, but the more elaborate ones require quite a lot of practice and skill, and you have to be very careful to avoid getting the strings tangled.

We are going to make some very simple marionettes – and because their movements would naturally be jerky and funny, let's design a family of ragged scarecrows. Then we can really have fun creating the different characters by emphasizing all the untidy and amusing features a scarecrow might have. Just like real scarecrows, they're improvized from all kinds of household and waste materials – such as raffia, old stockings and toilet-roll tubes.

THE BASIC FIGURE

Materials:

Old stocking (preferably stretch)
Toilet- or kitchen-roll inner tube
Skein of natural-coloured raffia
Hank of garden raffia
Scrap of black felt
Small cork or wooden bead for the nose
Red stranded embroidery cotton
Kapok or cotton wool
$\frac{1}{2}$in. square balsa wood
2 9in. lengths of balsa at least 1in. wide by $\frac{1}{4}$in. thick
Staples and a small screw eye
Black linen carpet thread
Wooden beads or small curtain rings (optional)
Evo-stik clear adhesive

Method for Cornelius or Clara (the adult marionettes): Turn your stocking to the wrong side and cut off the foot just above the heel. Tie tightly 6in. above the cut end. Push the stuffing up the cut end to make the head, adding enough until it is the size of a tennis ball: then tie the stocking tightly again, under the stuffing. Now bring the top of the stocking smoothly down over the head, pushing the remainder through a $4\frac{1}{2}$in. length of cardboard tube: then bring the top of the stocking up, round the outside of the tube, and tie it round the neck. Turn the remainder of the stocking down over the tube again (stuffing the end inside, if necessary).

Cut four 2in. lengths of $\frac{1}{2}$in. square balsa wood for the arms. Sandpaper smooth. For the hands, wind good quality raffia twelve times round a 3in. deep piece of card. Slide off and tie at the centre with 4in. of raffia. Cut the loops, then fold in half and bind close under the tied centre to hold together. To assemble, drive a staple into each end of one piece of wood, and into *one* end of a second piece: then link another staple through one of those on the first piece, before driving it into the free end of the second piece. Using strong thread or double cotton, stitch the staple at one end loosely to the top of the stocking-covered tube. Stitch the other arm to the opposite side of the body. Wait until the puppet is dressed and then tie the hands to the ends of the arms.

For the legs, cut two $2\frac{1}{2}$in lengths of wood and sandpaper smooth. Then wind raffia twelve times round a 9in. deep piece of card, and make the lower part of the leg as instructed for the hand. Drive staples into each end of

38

the wood, and stitch to the lower edge of the tube at each side of the body. Tie the raffia lower legs to the staples at the knee.

Follow individual instructions for the hair: then stick a cork, or stitch a bead, to the centre of the face for the nose. Cut circles in black felt for the eyes, and stick. Embroider mouth in stem stitch, using six strands of embroidery cotton.

CORNELIUS

Cornelius is at the back on the right in the picture opposite.

Materials:

The basic figure
Piece of fabric 4in. by 9in. for his shirt
10in. square of fabric for his trousers
Piece of felt 9in. by 18in. for his coat
9in. square of felt for his hat
$\frac{1}{4}$yd. of 1in. wide ribbon
Narrow round elastic

Method: Follow instructions for the basic figure, using a small cork for the nose, and $\frac{5}{8}$in. diameter circles for the eyes. For his beard, make a looped fringe from garden raffia: wind a length round three fingers, slide off and on to a thick piece of raffia: stitch securely into position with raffia. Continue to add looped lengths (about five in all) until the "fringe" measures 3in. Then stitch the top edge round the face as illustrated and trim the loops along the lower edge. Wrap lengths of garden raffia round an 8in. deep piece of card for the hair (the number depends on the thickness). Slide off and tie loosely at the centre, then stitch to the top of the head. Cut the loops and catch down all round his head.

Cut the fabric for his shirt 5in. deep by 4in. wide for the front, and a 5in. square for the back. With right sides together, join the side seams for 2½in. from the lower edge. Slit centre back. Join the shoulder seams for 1½in.

The ragged scarecrows: Cornelius, Clara and Hayseed

from each side edge. Turn in and hem the neck and sleeve edges. Turn to the right side, fit on puppet and slip-stitch centre back edges together.

Cut two pieces of fabric 10in. deep by 5in. wide for his trousers. Fold each piece of fabric in half lengthways, right side inside, and join the sides for 6in. from the lower edge. Now join the two pieces, right sides together, along the remainder of the sides, to form front and back seams of trousers. Turn the top edge under ½in. and thread elastic through. Turn to the right side, fit on puppet and draw up elastic round waist. Fray lower edges and tie round legs over the knee joint.

Draw a pattern for his coat from Fig. 41. Cut the front and sleeves twice and the back

39

once, *placing the broken line on the pattern to the centre back fold.* With the right sides together, join the front pieces to the back at the shoulders for 1in. from each side edge. Set the top of each sleeve into the armhole, matching sides, and the centre to the shoulder seam, easing gently round the curve. Join the side and sleeve seams. Turn to the right side. Turn back lapels and catch down. Cut two pockets 1in. by 1½in.: turn over ½in. for top flap on each, and catch down. Then stitch into position as indicated on the pattern. Sew a contrasting patch roughly on to the sleeve, as illustrated. Cut a 3½in. square of silk or soft fabric for his handkerchief: tuck into pocket and catch in position.

Tie the ribbon loosely round his neck to form a bow tie.

Draw a 5in. diameter circle for his hat, then rule a line ½in. below the centre (see Fig. 42): cut away the smaller (shaded) section, and then use as a pattern to cut the crown twice in felt. Cut a 6in. diameter circle, with a 3in. diameter hole in the centre, for the brim. Join the two crown pieces all round the curved edge: then turn to the right side and stitch the lower edge round the inner edge of the brim, right sides together. Fit on puppet as illustrated, tucking a sprig of dried foliage into the crown. String the head, back, hands and knees.

CLARA

Clara is the marionette on the left at the back in the picture on page 39.

Materials:

The basic figure
10in. square of fabric for her pants
¼yd. 36in. wide fabric for her dress
Piece of fabric 5in. deep by 6in. wide for her apron
9in. square of felt for her hat
Everlasting or artificial flowers
Wooden beads

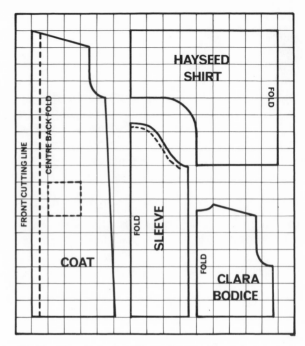

Fig 41. Cornelius's coat, Hayseed's shirt, Clara's bodice. One square = ½in.

Fig 42. Cornelius's hat

Stiff card
½yd. white tape
Narrow round elastic
Copydex adhesive

Method: Follow instructions for the basic figure, using a smaller cork than Cornelius's for the nose, and ⅝in. diameter circles for the eyes. For her hair, wind some garden raffia round an 8in. deep piece of card: slide off and tie at the centre. Stitch centre to the top of her head (using raffia), then bring the sides down and round to the back to form a bun, catching

40

firmly into position.

To make her pants, follow the directions for Cornelius's trousers.

Draw the bodice and sleeve patterns for her dress from Fig. 41. Cut the bodice and sleeve twice each: then slit one bodice piece up the centre to form two back pieces. Cut a piece of fabric 8in. deep by 16in. wide for the skirt. With the right sides of the bodice together, join the front to the back pieces at each shoulder. Gather the top edge of the sleeves, as indicated, then set into the armholes, drawing up the gathers to fit and distributing them evenly round the curve. Then join the sleeve and side seams. Gather the top edge of the skirt, then draw up and pin round the lower edge of the bodice, right sides together, distributing the gathers evenly before stitching to the top. Join the centre back seam of the skirt, leaving open for 2in. below the waist. Turn to the right side and fit on puppet. Gather sleeves $\frac{1}{2}$in. above lower edge and draw up round her wrists. Slip-stitch centre back seam.

Cut the apron fabric 5in. deep by 6in. wide. Gather the top edge and draw up to measure 4in. Stitch the gathered edge behind an 18in. length of tape, centres matching. Fray the edges, and add a patch, as illustrated. Then tie round her waist.

Cut a 5in. diameter circle of card, with a 2½in. diameter hole in the centre, for her hat. Stick the card to felt and cut out, with the edges of felt and card level. Stick the other side of the card to the felt, and cut again. Stitch the hat securely to the top of her head, then stick everlasting or artificial flowers all over the crown of the head, as illustrated.

Tie wooden beads round her neck.

String the head, back, hands and knees.

HAYSEED

Hayseed is the child marionette on the left in the picture above.

The ragged scarecrows: Cornelius and Clara, with their children (from left to right) *Hayseed, Baby Parsnip, and Harebell*

Materials:

The basic figure (see below)
9in. square of fabric for his shirt
Piece of fabric 5½in. by 10in. for his trousers
Strip of fabric 2in. by 9in. for his scarf
Narrow round elastic

Method: Follow instructions for the basic figure, but cut the cardboard tube 3in. long only: make the upper arms and legs 1½in. long, and make the lower arms by wrapping raffia twelve times round a 4in. deep card, and the lower legs twelve times round a 5in. deep card. Cut a small cork in half and use the tip for his nose. Cut $\frac{5}{8}$in. diameter circles of felt for his eyes. For his hair, wrap one or two strands of garden raffia round a 4in. deep card: slide off and tie at the centre, then fold in half and stitch to the top of his head, catching the looped ends over the face as illustrated. Wrap several more strands round a 5in. deep card: slide off and tie loosely at the centre, then stitch to the top of the head behind the first piece, catching the loops down loosely all round the sides and back of the head.

41

Cut two pieces of fabric 5½in. deep by 5in. wide for his trousers. Then follow the instructions for Cornelius, joining each leg for only 1½in. from the lower edge (instead of 6in.).

Draw a pattern for his shirt from Fig. 41. Cut twice. With the right sides together, join the two pieces along the top edge of each sleeve and shoulder, leaving 1in. open at the centre for the neck. Cut one piece in half for the centre back opening. Join the side and under sleeve seams, clip the curve and turn to the right side. Fit on puppet and slip-stitch the centre back seam together. Knot a strip of colourful fabric round his neck for his scarf.

String the head, back and hands.

HAREBELL

Harebell is the child marionette on the right, in the front, in the picture on page 41.

Materials:

Basic figure (see below)
Piece of fabric 10in. by 12in. for her dress
8in. square of silky fabric for her headscarf

Method: Follow directions for Hayseed, but use a wooden ball for her nose, and cut $\frac{7}{16}$in. diameter circles for her eyes. For her hair, wind a few strands of garden raffia round a 5in. deep card: slide off and tie loosely at the centre. Stitch to the top of her head as illustrated, then bring the loops smoothly down at each side and catch to the head. Trim neatly.

Cut two strips of fabric 2in. deep by 10in. wide for the yoke of her dress, and a piece 6in. by 12in. for her skirt. With the right sides together, join the two yoke strips along one edge, stitching 4½in. from each end, to leave 1in. open at the centre for neck. Now join the other edge, stitching 3in. from each end, for the under sleeve seams. Slit one piece in half for the centre back opening. Gather the top edge of the skirt, then, right sides together, pin round lower edge of the yoke, matching sides,

centre front, etc., so that the gathers are evenly distributed. Draw up to fit and stitch. Join the centre back seam of the skirt, leaving 1in. open below the yoke. Fit dress on puppet and slip-stitch the centre back seam.

Fold the headscarf into a triangle and tie round the hair as illustrated, catching to the head to hold in place.

String the head, back and hands.

BABY PARSNIP

Baby Parsnip is the child marionette in the middle, at the front, in the picture on page 41.

Materials:

Basic figure (see below)
Piece of fabric 5in. by 10in. for the dress
Piece of fabric 5in. by 2½in. for the bonnet
6in. 1½in.-wide lace
5in. 1in.-wide ribbon

Method: Follow instructions for the basic figure, cutting the tube only 2in. long, and stuffing any surplus stocking up inside it. No wood is used for the limbs: make the feet as directed for the adult hands; make arms as lower arms of Hayseed and Harebell. Knot the two ends of the raffia used for tying the centre, to form a small loop, then stitch the loops to the body to join the limbs as for the other figures. Use a wooden bead for the nose, and cut $\frac{7}{16}$in. diameter circles for the eyes. For the hair, wrap a strand of garden raffia round a 2in. deep card: slide off, tie at the centre, fold in half and stitch to the top of the head.

Fold the dress fabric in half to measure 5in. square (fold is centre front). Then fold again in the same direction to measure 5in. by 2½in. (forming sides): slit this second fold 1½in. down from the top edge, for armholes. Open out and stitch lace round armholes, joining cut edges at the top. With the right side inside, join the centre back seam of the dress, then gather the top edge, fit on puppet

42

and draw up round the neck.

Cut a 5in. diameter semi-circle of fabric for the bonnet. Gather round 1in. inside the curved edge. Then gather ¼in. inside the straight, lower edge. Fit bonnet on head and draw up the gathers round the neck and face. Tie the ribbon into a bow and stitch under the chin.

String the head and back.

Stringing your puppets

Cut two 9in. lengths of 1in.-wide wood: then cut one piece into two, measuring 6in. and 3in. Stick these two pieces across the longer piece, as shown in Fig. 43, equal at either side. Make holes at A, B and C, and attach a screw eye to the front as shown at D. Stitch one end of a length of carpet thread securely to the body of the puppet at each side of the head, back and knees: thread the other end through holes (A–head: B–back: C–legs) and secure– leaving about 18in. of thread–with a bead or curtain ring, etc. Adjust carefully until the balance is correct and the puppet hangs properly.

Finally, stitch a long thread to one wrist, thread through screw eye and stitch the other end to the other wrist, so that the hands hang by the sides.

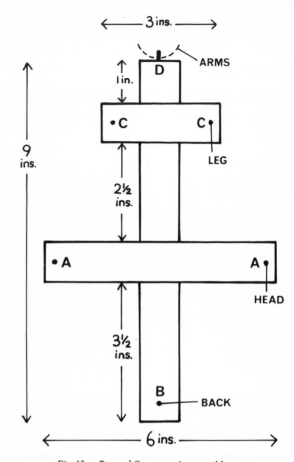

Fig 43.   Ragged Scarecrow's control bar

Miranda–the baby mermaid: a simple soft toy

Careful research for references from which to prepare your design is even more important with soft toys, because they lack the animation of puppets. Often it is necessary to emphasize and exaggerate specific characteristics to an even greater degree, as you will see from the varied examples which follow.

Our first toy is a very simple flat felt doll– though she doesn't *look* flat once she's made up. She is just the right size and shape for tiny hands to hold and play with and she has an appeal which a small child will instinctively feel makes her a friend.

In making a soft toy, the stuffing is very important. Use a good quality Kapok (foam chips can be substituted, but tend to be lumpy, and are never very satisfactory). And always remember to insert the stuffing a little at a time, pushing it well into the corners and round curves, following the shape of the toy all the time: you can spoil the whole effect by trying to hurry, and shoving large lumps of stuffing inside without pushing it down properly. The tips of your scissors and the end of a pencil can both be very helpful when pushing the stuffing into place.

Let's make our doll rather different–by giving her a fishy tail so that she becomes a mermaid: then she won't need any clothes, either–just a necklace of flowers. Look at the picture and see how her head, arms, hands, body and tail are all curved to emphasize the rounded shape of a small child.

To save time and trouble, you needn't appliqué the scales on to her tail: you can simply stick them into place with Copydex.

Materials:

9in. square of flesh pink felt
9in. square of emerald green felt
3in. square of pale sea green felt
3in. square of deep turquoise felt
3in. square of pale turquoise felt
Scraps of black felt for eyes
Golden-brown double-double knitting wool for hair
Red and black embroidery cottons
Small pink and blue guipure lace daisies–or alternative trimming
Kapok for stuffing
Copydex adhesive

To make your patterns: Trace separate pattern pieces for the front, back and tail from Fig. 44. For the front, follow the outer line round the head–then follow the inner line for the back.

Method: Cut the front and back once each in pink felt, and the tail twice in emerald. Mark notches and position of features on head pieces. Embroider the nose and mouth in the positions indicated, following the diagram for size. Trace the pattern (Fig. 45) for the eye twice. Tack to black felt, allowing a small area all round: cut each eye, pinking the edge of the circle *outside* the edge of the paper. Position the eyes accurately by pushing a pin through the centre of each, and then through the dot on the face: stitch or stick neatly all round the edge.

Now run a gathering thread all round the edge of the front of the head, between the lowest notch at each side. Then, with right sides together, pin the front of the head to the back, matching notches. Draw up the gathering thread to fit, and oversew the back and front together all round the outer edge, arms and body as well, leaving only the lower edge open. Oversew the two tail pieces together along each side, leaving the top and lower edges open. Now, with the right sides together, join the tail to the front of the body, so that (on the wrong side) the tail curves to the left. Turn both halves to the right side. Oversew the lower edges of the tail together neatly.

44

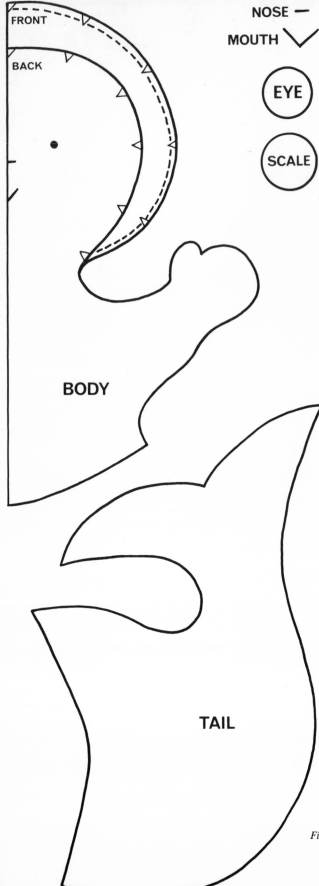

NOSE —

MOUTH ∨

FRONT

BACK

EYE

SCALE

BODY

TAIL

Fig 45. *Miranda: eye, nose, mouth, scale (to trace)*

Stuff the head, arms and body firmly: push a little stuffing right down to the tip of the tail, so that it is lightly padded, then increase the amount on the curve and stuff firmly above. Slip-stitch the tail to the back of the body, inserting a little more stuffing just before the end.

For the scales, cut about twenty $\frac{5}{8}$in. diameter circles of felt each in emerald, pale sea green, deep turquoise and pale turquoise. Pin a row of alternating deep and pale turquoise scales side-by-side over the body and tail join: appliqué the upper half of each to the body. Now pin a row of emerald and pale green scales below the turquoise, positioning them under and between the first row, so that the turquoise scales overlap the upper half of the second row, as illustrated. Then appliqué the lower halves of the top scales over the green ones below. Repeat, with another row of alternating turquoise scales, appliquéing the lower halves of the green scales over the upper halves of the turquoise. Continue to cover the tail in this manner round to the narrowest part of the curve, arranging so that you finish with a row of turquoise, the lower edges stitched to the tail.

For the hair, cut twenty 10in. long strands of wool (more or less according to thickness– double-double knitting wool is extra thick). Tie together at the centre with a short length of the wool. Stitch the centre securely to the top of the head, then catch loosely at each side, between the two lowest notches and round to the back. Cut ten 12in. long strands of wool (or half the previous quantity). Tie the wool in a loose knot at the centre, and then stitch the knot securely to the top of the head, behind and just overlapping the centre of the first piece. Catch both ends lightly across the back of the head.

Stitch lace daisies (or cut flowers from coloured felt), or alternative trimming to form a necklace, as illustrated, and in the hair, to mask the loops of wool, and hold the wool more securely in place.

Fig 44. *Miranda: body and tail (to trace)*

Emma-Kate: a rag doll for a little girl

Emma-Kate has long hair and big eyes and a whole wardrobe of clothes, all rather Victorian in style. She is what is known as a "rag doll", because she is made of plain cotton fabric: dolls made in this way have been popular for many, many centuries.

See how we emphasize her charm with a flower-trimmed poke bonnet and broderie anglaise pantalettes, romantically full-skirted dresses and an old-fashioned nightie. And although her features are so simple, they are carefully designed to give her a bright, happy expression.

Materials:

10in. of 36in. wide cream cotton poplin
Kapok for stuffing
Postcard or buckram
Scrap of black felt
Red and white embroidery cottons
Thick double-double knitting wool for hair
Copydex adhesive (optional)

To make your patterns: Rule a sheet of paper into **one-inch squares** (or use graph paper), and draw out your pattern following Fig. 46. There is *no* seam allowance on these pattern pieces, so *allow $\frac{1}{4}$in. turnings all round* (except on folds, of course): this is to ensure greater accuracy in more detailed areas.

Trace patterns for the features and shoe, from Fig. 47 and 48.

Method: Allowing $\frac{1}{4}$in. turnings all round (as above), cut the front and back once each in poplin, the arm and leg four times each, and the sole twice. Cut the sole twice more in thin card or buckram, slightly smaller than the pattern. Mark darts on the back of the head, and notches on the front and arms.

With the wrong side of the fabric facing you, pin and stitch the darts. Run a gathering thread round the front of the head, beginning and ending at the lowest notches. With the right sides together, pin the darts to correspond with the notches, then draw up the thread to fit, distributing the gathers evenly.

Making $\frac{1}{4}$in. seams, join the front to the back round the outer edge, leaving the lower

Emma-Kate

47

edge open. Trim seams and clip curves (especially at the neck), and turn to the right side.

To make each arm, stitch two pieces, right sides together, all round the outer edge, leaving open between the notches. Trim seams and clip curves (especially at wrist): turn to the right side. Stuff the hand and arm firmly, turn raw edges inside, and slip-stitch together.

To make each leg, stitch two pieces, right sides together, down each side, leaving the upper and lower edges open. Fit sole inside lower edge, matching centres at front and back to the seams, then stitch neatly into position. Trim and clip seams: turn to the right side. Push the card or buckram sole down the leg and fit it neatly inside the foot (hold in position temporarily at the back and front with a safety pin). Stuff the foot, and then the leg, firmly. Tack across the top, *placing the front and back seams together in the centre.*

Stuff the head firmly. Roll up a strip of card or buckram tightly so that it is about 2-3in. long and the thickness of a pencil: fit this inside the neck, to hold the head steady. Then continue stuffing – round the neck stiffening and then the body. Turn in and pin the raw lower edges, fit the tops of the legs inside, and stitch firmly across the front and back, inserting more stuffing into the body if necessary, before finally closing the seam.

Stitch the top of each arm (hand curving forward) to the tip of each shoulder (see points X marked on the pattern).

Cut the eyes in black felt, as illustrated – using pinking shears, and following the curved edge of the circle in Fig. 47 as the inner edge of the zig-zag: or cut V-shapes all the way round with embroidery scissors: or just cut circles – but make them slightly larger than the pattern. Embroider a white star in the centre of each eye, as shown, then stick into position with Copydex (or appliqué). Embroider the mouth with two straight stitches, in red.

For her hair, cut twelve 16in. lengths of double-double knitting wool (cut more if you are using a thinner wool – double-double is twice the thickness of ordinary double knitting wool). Catch matching cotton round the centre, then stitch securely to the front of the head, 1½in. in front of the seam, level with the centre dart. Cut another twelve 16in. lengths of wool: stitch just behind the first, 1in. in front of the seam. Repeat with another group ½in. in front of the seam, and a fourth group over it. Then cut only ten 16in. lengths to stitch over the dart. Behind this stitch ten 15in. lengths, then ten 14in. lengths – and, finally, ten 12in. lengths.

Draw the first, front group of twelve smoothly down over each side of the face, as shown, and catch lightly to the head over the lowest dart. Then draw back the second group and catch at each side over the centre dart. Smooth the hair down all round, and trim the ends evenly.

Emma-Kate's clothes

To make your patterns: For greater accuracy, Emma-Kate's clothes are drawn to a finer scale, so rule your paper into **half-inch squares** to draw your patterns from Fig. 49. And again, *no turnings are allowed,* so cut an extra ¼in. on all pattern pieces (except on folds), unless otherwise instructed – or when actual measurements are stated.

Striped Dress

Materials:

¼yd. of 36in.-wide dress cotton
Bias binding to match
Shirring elastic
3 snap fasteners
Lace flower to trim

Method: Cut the bodice front once, the back twice and the sleeve twice – allowing ¼in. turnings everywhere except round the neck edge on the bodice. Cut a piece of fabric 6½in. deep by 18in. wide for the skirt.

With the right sides together, join the front and back bodice pieces at the shoulders. Gather round the top of each sleeve, as indicated. Then, right sides together, set sleeves into armholes, distributing the gathers evenly. Now join the sleeve and side seams, and turn up a 1¼in. deep hem round the lower edge of each sleeve: then make another line of stitches, ¼in. below the first row, to form a channel.

Gather along the top edge of the skirt. Then, right sides together, join to the lower edge of the bodice, matching sides and centres, and distributing the gathers evenly between. Join the centre back seam of the skirt to within 2in. of the waist, for opening.

Turn under a narrow hem down each side

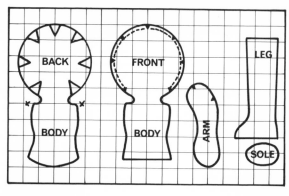

Fig 46.   Emma Kate: body. One square=1in.

Fig 48.   Emma-Kate: shoe (to trace)

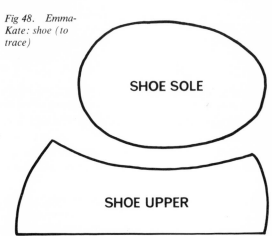

Fig 47.   Emma-Kate: features (to trace)

Fig 49.   Emma-Kate: dress, cape, bonnet, nightgown. One square=½in.

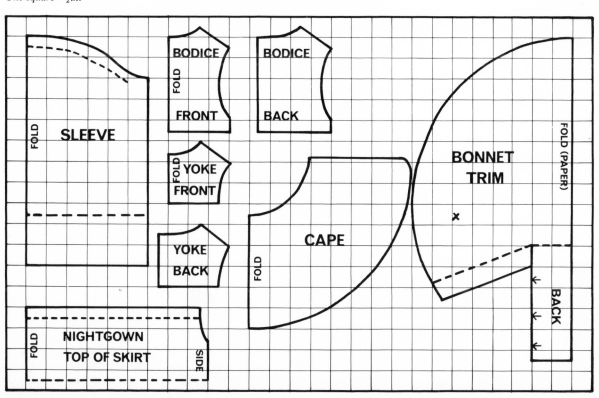

of the centre back opening, and bind the neck edge neatly.

Trim, clip and press all seams, then turn to the right side.

Fit dress on the doll to mark the length: turn up the hem, stitch snap fasteners on back opening, and thread elastic through the sleeve channels and draw up to fit wrists.

Stitch flower trim at front neck, over the binding.

Pantalettes

Materials:

Piece of white fabric 7in. deep by 12in. wide
12in. of $1\frac{1}{4}$in.-deep broderie anglaise
12in. narrow ribbon (if using slotted broderie anglaise)
Narrow round elastic

Method: Cut two pieces of fabric 7in. deep by 6in. wide. If using slotted broderie anglaise, thread ribbon through the holes. Then stitch trimming along the lower edge of each piece (turn up a narrow hem first, if the fabric is liable to fray).

Fold each piece in half lengthways, right side inside: join the side seam of each leg for 5in. from the lower edge. Now, right sides together, join the two pieces along the remainder of these seams up to the top edge, to form centre front and back seams.

Turn over a $\frac{1}{2}$in. hem along the top edge, thread elastic through, and draw up to fit waist.

Easter Bonnet

Materials:

$8\frac{1}{2}$in. diameter circles of two contrasting fabrics
$8\frac{1}{2}$in. diameter circle of hat or pelmet buckram
$\frac{5}{8}$yd. $\frac{1}{2}$in.-wide ruched braid
$\frac{1}{2}$yd. $\frac{1}{2}$in.-wide ribbon
Forget-me-nots to trim
Copydex adhesive

Method: Trace pattern on to folded grease-proof paper: open out and cut in buckram (no turnings needed).

If using pelmet buckram, iron the inner fabric on to one side (using a very damp cloth to make it adhere). Then cut the fabric away all round, level with the edge of the buckram. Iron the outer fabric on to the other side of the buckram in the same way, and cut this level with the edge also, *but leave a $\frac{1}{2}$in. overlap down each side of the back* (see arrows). Turn this surplus fabric over and stick to the inside.

If you are *not* using adhesive pelmet buckram, follow the above directions, tacking each fabric all round, close to the edge, stretching it smoothly over the buckram. Or, if the fabric you are using is not too thin, you can stick it to the buckram.

Stick braid over the raw lower edge of the back, and all round the curved edge of the brim, so that the lower edge of the back overlaps the brim about $\frac{1}{2}$in., allowing the bonnet to bend over across the top of the back (see broken lines on the pattern).

Cut ribbon in half for ties, and stitch each to inside of brim at X. Then trim the outside of the brim with forget-me-nots, as illustrated,

Emma-Kate's nightdress

50

covering the stitches attaching the ribbons.

Matching Cape and Bag

Materials:

9in. square of felt
4in. length ½in.-wide ruched braid
⅜yd. 1in.- or 1¼in.-wide lace
4in. Russian braid or cord
Hook and eye

Method: Cut the cape once in felt (no turnings are required). Gather close to the neck edge, and draw up to fit doll. Then stitch neatly to one edge of the braid, to form a narrow stand-up collar, as illustrated. Stitch hook and eye to ends of braid, for neck fastening.

Cut a 4in. diameter circle of felt for the bag. Using a tiny gathering stitch, join the straight edge of the lace all round, level with the edge of the felt (the outer edge of the lace towards the centre of the circle). Draw up the gathers tightly and secure.

Stitch the two ends of the Russian braid or cord just inside, to form a looped handle.

Shoes

Materials:

Piece of felt 5in. by 4in.
Thin card (optional)

Method: Cut the upper four times and the sole twice in felt as Fig. 48 (no turnings are necessary).

For each shoe, oversew two uppers together, right sides inside, at the back and front. Turn to the right side and oversew the lower edge of the upper to the sole, wrong sides together, matching seams at centre front and back.

To stiffen the sole, cut card slightly smaller than the pattern, and stick inside each shoe.

Flowered Nightgown

Materials:

¼yd. 36in.-wide fabric
Bias binding
Shirring elastic
2 snap fasteners
6in. narrow ribbon

Method: Cut the yoke front once, and the back and sleeve twice each–allowing ¼in. turnings everywhere except round the neck edges on the yoke. Cut two pieces of fabric 9in. deep by 9in. wide for the skirt: *then* cut armholes at each side of these two pieces by folding each piece in half lengthways and placing the pattern for the top of the skirt level with the top, side and folded edges. Slit the fold for 2½in. below the waist on one piece only, for centre back opening.

With the right sides together, join the front and back yoke pieces at the shoulders. Gather the top edge of the skirt front: then, right sides together, join it to the lower edge of the yoke front, matching sides and centres, and distributing the gathers evenly between. Gather the top edges of the skirt back, and join to each side of the yoke in the same way.

Gather round the top of each sleeve. Then, right sides together, set into the armholes, distributing the gathers evenly all round. Now join the side and sleeve seams: turn up a 1¼in. deep hem round the lower edge of each sleeve, then make another line of stitches ¼in. below the first row, to form a channel.

Turn under a narrow hem down each side of the centre back opening, and bind the neck edge neatly.

Trim, clip and press all seams, then turn to the right side.

Fit nightdress on the doll to mark the length: turn up the hem. Stitch snap fasteners at back opening, and thread elastic through the sleeve channels, and draw up to fit wrists.

Tie the ribbon into a bow, and stitch to the centre front of the neck, as illustrated.

A Warren of Rabbits: a complete family of soft toys

If you compare the parent rabbits and their children in the photograph, you can see the differences which distinguish them. The parents *aren't,* as you can see, just a larger version of the babies: they are much leaner, with longer ears in proportion to their size, more pointed noses and slightly harrassed expressions. Whilst the young ones are plump and round, with very small paws and a wide-eyed look of surprise at everything they see in the world around them. And see how a waistcoat and a check apron tell us immediately who is father and who is mother. It is little things like these which will make *your* toys distinctive and appealing.

It doesn't matter if you can't get Acrilan fleece (it's the kind of soft, fluffy material used for dressing gowns): just use a soft fabric or felt instead. But do *try* to use the fleece if you can, because it stretches slightly, and is most effective for moulding softly rounded faces and bodies.

PARENT RABBIT

Materials:

$\frac{3}{8}$yd. mid-brown velveteen 36in. wide
Piece of white Acrilan fleece about 16in. square
Piece of pale pink brushed cotton about 8in. square
Piece of buckram about 9in. square
Scrap of pink felt for the nose
Scraps of light and dark blue, or yellow and brown felt for the eyes
Scrap of white fur or swansdown for the tail
Kapok for stuffing
Black stranded embroidery cotton

To make your pattern: Rule a sheet of paper into **one-inch squares** (or use graph paper), and draw out the pattern pieces from Fig. 50 for the parent rabbit. Trace the features from Fig. 51.

Rule a sheet of paper into **half-inch squares,** and draw out the waistcoat from the separate diagram, Fig. 54.

Method: Cut the head gusset and base once each, and the side and ear twice each, all in brown velveteen. Cut the front once, and the head twice in white Acrilan. Cut the ear twice more in pink cotton. Then cut the ear stiffening twice in buckram (keep the remaining buckram to stiffen the base).

With the right sides of the head together, and making $\frac{1}{4}$in. turnings, join the two pieces between the nose and the front of the neck. Then place the rounded end of the head gusset to the tip of the nose, and stitch evenly round each side of the head, right sides together, ending at the back of the neck. Turn to the right side.

*With the right sides together, join the front to each side piece between the front of the neck and tip of the foot. Join the back seam, leaving open between X's. Stitch the head carefully into position, matching centres at front and back.

Cut a piece of buckram slightly smaller than the base, and tack to the wrong side. Then pin the base evenly to the lower edge of the body and stitch. Turn to the right side. Stuff firmly, and oversew the back opening neatly.

To make the ears, stitch a velvet and a pink cotton piece together all round the curved edge, the right sides inside. Trim and clip seam, then turn to the right side and insert buckram stiffening. Turn in the raw edges and stitch along the base, gathering slightly. Then stitch firmly into position at the back of the head, following the illustration closely.

Cut the eye twice in pale blue or yellow felt, the pupils in deep blue or brown, and the nose in pink. Appliqué the eyes to the side of the head, with the pupils in the centre, and then stem-stitch round the outer edge with black embroidery cotton.

Appliqué the nose into position, the rounded top just overlapping the tip of the brown gusset.

Make the tail from fur or swansdown (or make a pompon from white wool), and stitch firmly into place at the base of the back seam.

Mother's apron is simply a piece of check gingham 12in. by 5in., hemmed on three sides and gathered into a waistband 5in. long. Stitch a length of ribbon at each side and tie at the back.

For Father's waistcoat you need a piece of felt 28in. by 12in. Cut the front twice and the back once.

Join the centre front, lapping one side over the other. Stitch tiny lace flowers down the front for buttons. With the edges overlapping, stitch the front to the back along one shoulder and side. Then fit the waistcoat on the rabbit and join the remaining shoulder and side seams in the same way.

BABY RABBIT

Materials:

Piece of light brown velveteen 14in. by 8in.
Piece of white Acrilan fleece 7in. by 8in.
Piece of pale pink brushed cotton 3in. by 4in.
Piece of buckram 3in. by 4in.
Scrap of pink felt for the nose
Scrap of white, blue, and green or brown felt for the eyes
Small daisy for the tail (or as parent rabbit)
Forget-me-nots or lace flowers for trimming
Kapok for stuffing
Black stranded embroidery cotton

To make your pattern: **Rule** a sheet of paper into **half-inch squares** (or use graph paper), and draw out the pattern pieces from Fig. 52 for the baby rabbit. Trace the features from Fig. 53.

Method: Cut the head gusset and base once each, and the side and ear twice each, in brown velveteen. Cut the front once and the head

Family of rabbits

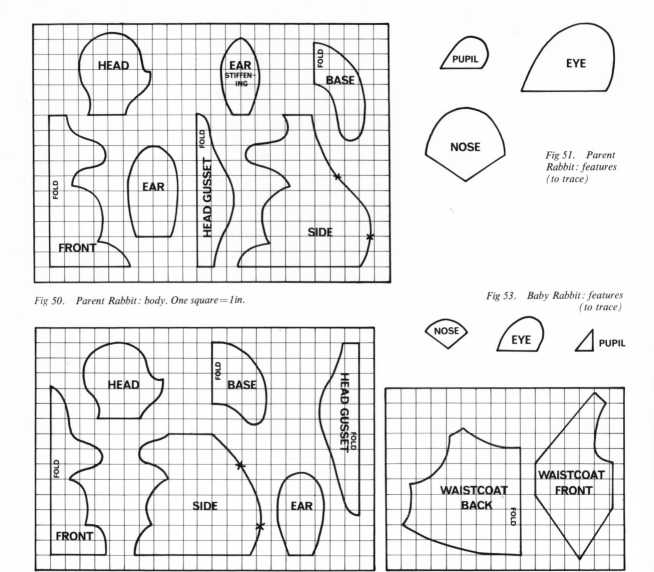

Fig 50. *Parent Rabbit: body. One square=1in.*

Fig 51. *Parent Rabbit: features (to trace)*

Fig 53. *Baby Rabbit: features (to trace)*

Fig 52. *Baby Rabbit: body. One square=½in.*

Fig 54. *Parent Rabbit: waistcoat. One square=½in.*

twice in white Acrilan. Cut the ear twice more in pink cotton.

With the right sides of the head together, join at the tip of the nose. Then place the rounded end of the head gusset to the tip of the nose and, making ¼in. seams, stitch evenly round each side of the head, right sides together, ending at the back of the neck.

Now place the pointed top of the front to the tip of the nose and, right sides together, join to each side of the head between the nose and front of the neck. Turn to the right side.

Now continue as directed for the parent rabbit (from*), omitting the stiffening in the ears, cutting the eyes in white felt, with coloured pupils, and substituting a daisy for the fluffy tail. Wind tiny flowers into a garland and stitch to the centre of the head, or round one ear, or in a spray at the side of the neck.

54

How animals differ: Squirrels

Compare the squirrels in this section with the rabbits in the last, and you will see how basically the same shape of toy can assume completely different identities by small, but important, changes of detail. You can see from the patterns how similar the bodies and heads are: but notice that the squirrel's front paws are close together, his nose is a different shape, he has small, pointed ears and, of course, that enormous, bushy tail. These are all points to be brought out and exaggerated in the design of your soft toy.

This basic body position is a useful one for many soft toys: it is a compact, easy shape for a small child to clutch and handle, and it sits up steadily on its own, without tending to fall over all the time. By changing the shape slightly, and the colour, and adding appropriate features, you could turn it into a dog or a cat or a bear or a panda, a lion or even a mouse.

Glossy, golden-brown velvet makes a beautiful coat for your squirrel, but any soft fabric or felt, would do. And although the squirrels in the picture have tails of thick-cut furnishing fringe, they would be lovely in fur or fur fabric, if you have a small piece; or you could make the tail from wool like the glove puppet squirrel (page 9): just be sure to make it thick and bushy.

Materials (for each):

Piece of golden-brown velvet 9in. by 27in.
Piece of white Acrilan fleece 7½in. by 10in.
Scrap of black felt
Scrap of white felt
1½yd. of ¾in. deep, thick-cut cushion fringe
Kapok for stuffing
Stiff card or buckram
Copydex adhesive (optional)

To make your pattern: Rule a sheet of paper into **half-inch squares** (or use graph paper), and draw out your pattern pieces following Fig. 55. For greater accuracy, *turnings are not allowed* on the patterns, *so add another ¼in. all round* (except on folds), when cutting out. Trace the features from Fig. 56.

Method: Allowing ¼in. turnings all round (as above), cut the head, body and ear twice, and the head gusset and base once each, in velvet. Cut the front once and the ear twice more, in Acrilan. Cut the base again in card or buckram, *slightly smaller than the pattern.*

With the right sides together, join the two head pieces between the tip of the nose and the front of the neck. Then place the point of the gusset to the tip of the nose, and stitch to each side of the head, right sides together, ending at the back of the neck. Turn head on to the right side.

With the right sides together, join the front of the body to each side between the front of the neck and tip of the foot (match curves and corners, and pin at these points, for exactness). Join the sides down the centre back seam.

Stitch the head carefully into position, right sides together, matching centre of gusset to back seam, and front seam of head to centre of body front. Clip and, if necessary, oversew all seams, particularly reinforcing sharp turns.

Pin the base into position, matching centre fronts, centre back to the back seam, and notches at front of feet to seams joining front to sides of body. Now stitch the base to the body, *only* round the front half of the toy, leaving the back open between the circles. Trim seam and turn to the right side.

Roll the body back to the neck and stuff the head firmly: then proceed down the body, stuffing the paws carefully, until the body is two-thirds stuffed. Insert card or buckram base (stick to fabric base with a little Copydex

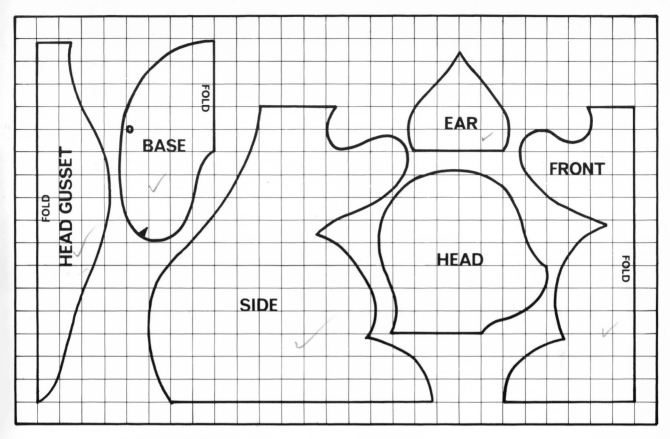

Fig 55. Nutty Squirrels: body. One square=½in.

Fig 56. Nutty Squirrels: features (to trace)

to hold in position). Complete stuffing the remainder of the body and the feet, then turn in the raw edges, re-pin the base to the body and slip-stitch the opening neatly together.

To make each ear, stitch a brown and white piece together, right sides inside, leaving the lower straight edge open. Trim the seam and clip the corner neatly, then turn to the right side. Turn the raw lower edges under and slip-stitch together. Fold the ear down the centre, white inside, and stitch neatly into position at the side of the head, following the illustration for guidance.

To make the tail, measure fringe 8½in. from one end, then fold over and stitch alongside next 8½in., oversewing the top edges together firmly. Fold the fringe back round the cut end and oversew again, alongside the double thickness. Turn again, and continue to stitch side-by-side until you have six thicknesses of fringe, finishing the cut end off neatly. Curl one end round and catch to the inside, as illustrated. Stitch the other end firmly to the base of the body, over the back seam, and then catch the tail itself to the body.

Cut the eye twice in white felt, and the pupils and nose in black. Stick or appliqué into position, following the illustration carefully.

To make Mrs Squirrel's apron, cut a piece of check gingham 3½in. deep by 6in. wide. Turn under a narrow hem along the sides and base, and gather the top edge. Then stitch one edge of a 12in. length of ½in. wide ribbon over the gathers on the right side of the apron, matching centres. Trim the top edge, fold the ribbon over, and stitch the other edge over the gathers on the wrong side.

Christopher Donkey: standing on four legs

Now for a completely different shape: a *standing* instead of a *sitting,* animal. This donkey is a good example of a basic shape which can be adapted to make anything from a horse to a puppy, a tiger to a giraffe. It just depends, as always, on collecting your reference, studying it hard, and then emphasizing all the characteristics of the particular animal you are designing.

In this case, it is the arched neck, long ears, thick mane, big soft eyes and slightly awkward legs which make our animal so unmistakably recognizable as a young donkey. If you want to give him straw panniers like the ones in the picture, make them by oversewing several strands of raffia round and round, shaping them into deep baskets, as illustrated. Then join them with a length of decorative ribbon.

Materials:

$\frac{5}{8}$yd. of 36in.-wide fabric (*or* $\frac{1}{2}$yd. of 48in. or 54in.-wide fabric)
9in. square of black felt
Piece of pink felt 7in. by 8in.
Piece of buckram or Vilene 7in. by 8in.
Scraps of golden-brown and white felt for the eyes
Double-double knitting wool for the mane
Kapok for stuffing
Stiff card
Copydex adhesive (optional)

To make your pattern: Rule a sheet of paper into **one-inch squares** and draw out the pattern pieces, following Fig. 57. Trace the eye in three parts (Fig. 58): first the whole area, then the centre and lower sections, and finally the lower section only.

Method: Cut the body, inside legs and outer ear twice each, and the head gusset and tail once each, in fabric. Cut the inner ear twice in pink felt, the two foot pieces twice each, and the two hoof pieces four times each, in black felt. Then cut the outer ear twice more in buckram or Vilene, $\frac{1}{4}$in. smaller all round than the pattern.

With the right side of the fabric facing, tack a front and a back hoof to both the body pieces and both the inside leg pieces—the top edge of the hoof level with the broken line on the pattern: appliqué the felt to the fabric along this line.

Now, with the right sides together, stitch an inside leg piece to each side of the body, joining between points A–B, C–D and E–F. Then join the two inside leg pieces from A–F. Join the chest from A–G. With right sides together, stitch the head gusset to each side of the head, matching points G and H. Then join the body between F and J, finishing off securely. Trim seams and clip curves, then turn to the right side.

Stuff firmly, pushing well down into the nose, back and tops of the legs: stuff each leg from the bottom, and close temporarily with a pin when nearly full. To complete each leg, pin a foot to the lower edge of the hoof, centres matching at front and back (arrows indicate the front): oversew neatly along one side of the hoof. Now cut the foot again, in card, a fraction smaller than the pattern. Slip the card inside and then continue oversewing the base to half-way along the other side of the hoof: complete stuffing before finishing oversewing.

When the body and head are fully stuffed, turn under the raw edges and pin sides of neck together. Beginning at point J, slip-stitch the neck seam, inserting more stuffing before finally closing the opening at the top.

To make the mane, begin at the top point of the head gusset, H, and mark with a pin every half inch down the back neck seam, making fourteen in all. Now, starting at the

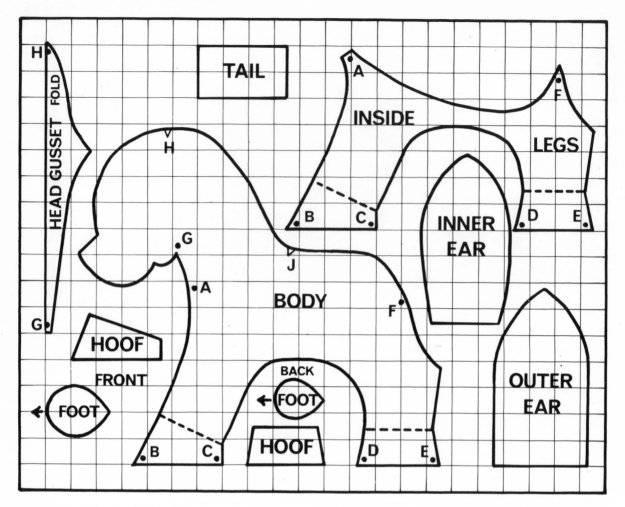

Fig 57. Christopher Donkey: body. One square=1in.

Fig 58. Christopher Donkey: eye (to trace)

lowest pin, nearest point J, make a couple of stitches across the seam to secure cotton. Then cut a piece of card $\frac{1}{2}$in. deep by about 5-6in. wide, and wind the wool evenly round it ten times. Keeping the wool on the card, slip

your needle through the loops, draw up tightly along one edge of the card, and then take another stitch across the seam: repeat several times, so that the wool is firmly attached, then cut the loops neatly along the opposite edge of the card.

Continue in this manner right up the back seam, at each marked point, altering the depth of the card, and number of times the wool is wound round it, as follows:

Wind wool ten times round 1in.-deep card twice.

Wind wool ten times round 1$\frac{1}{2}$in.-deep card once.

Wind wool fifteen times round 1$\frac{1}{2}$in.-deep card twice.

> Wind wool twenty times round 2in.-deep card eight times.

Now make six more pin-marks at $\frac{1}{2}$in. intervals down the centre of the front gusset, and then complete the mane as follows:

> Wind wool twenty times round 2in.-deep card four times.

> Wind wool twenty times round 1$\frac{1}{2}$in.-deep card once.

> Wind wool twenty times round 1in.-deep card once.

Trim where necessary.

Tack the buckram or Vilene stiffening to the wrong side of each outer ear piece, the fabric overlapping all round. Then turn the fabric up over the stiffening along the lower edge, and tack to form a narrow hem. With right sides together, join the outer ears to the inner ear pieces, *matching cut edges,* leaving the base open. Trim and clip seams, then turn to the right side. Press. Fold the ear in half lengthways, felt inside, and stitch the lower edge to each side of the head, as illustrated, continuing about $\frac{3}{4}$in. up the front edges, to hold the ears upright.

Turn under and tack a narrow hem along one side and both ends of the tail. Wind wool fifteen times round a 2in. deep card, then tie the loops together securely with a short length of wool: now tie this "tassel" to the centre of four 8in. lengths of wool. Fold *this* wool in half, to make eight thicknesses, and wrap the fabric tightly round it, raw edge inside, one short end close to the top of the tassel: slip-stitch edge along length of tail. Cut the excess wool away at the top, just inside the fabric, and stitch the top of the tail firmly to the body as illustrated. Finally, stitch the top of the tassel securely to the end of the tail.

Cut the whole eye pattern in white felt, the second pattern in golden brown and the smallest in black, for the pupil. Stick or sew the brown over the white and the black over the brown, before either sticking or appliqué-ing into position on each side of the head, as in the illustration.

Merrybell the Jester: a patchwork version of an old favourite

For our final soft toy, we look to the past. You are sure to have seen jesters dressed in gaily coloured costumes in pictures of festive occasions centuries ago. The jester was always the court favourite, and played a specially important part in the Christmas celebrations and tradition. They wore strange, pointed hats, and had bells sewn all over their clothes so that they jingled merrily as they leapt and danced about, making everyone aware of their presence. Often, they carried a small model replica of themselves on a stick, which they waved high in the air as they entertained the company with their antics.

As the jesters of old were intended to amuse people, so our modern one is meant for just the same purpose. He is on a stick, too, with a brightly coloured patchwork costume and lots of silver bells. He would make a lovely rattle for a baby–but in that case, be sure to sew the bells on very, *very* firmly, so that they can't possibly be chewed off: or, safer still, put a couple of bells into a small plastic pill container and sew it inside the body when you are stuffing the toy. Then, with no bells on the outside, you can be sure of avoiding dangerous accidents.

Now that you have seen how to make such a wide variety of puppets and soft toys, you are probably full of ideas for designs of your own. Just remember the basic rules, and you are sure to produce some exciting results of which you can be justly proud.

Materials:

9in. square of olive green felt
9in. square of canary yellow felt
6in. square of deep pink felt
6in. square of mauve felt blue
4in. square of flesh pink felt red
Scrap of black felt
6in. square of buckram
Red embroidery cotton
Kapok for stuffing
9in. long wooden spoon (optional)
11 tiny silver bells (from haberdashery stores or pet shops)
Copydex adhesive (optional)

To make your pattern: Rule a sheet of paper into **half-inch squares** (or use graph paper), and draw out the pattern pieces following Fig. 59.

Trace the face, hand and diamond shape from Fig. 60.

Method: Cut the body once, the leg twice, the sole once, and the diamond four times, in green felt. Repeat in yellow felt. Cut the arm and the shoe twice each, and the diamond four times, in deep pink. Repeat in mauve felt. Cut the face once and the hand four times, in flesh felt. Cut the head only down to the broken line, slightly smaller than the pattern, in buckram.

All the seams are joined by oversewing the two edges neatly together *on the right side* with black cotton, and then oversewing back again, crossing the previous line of stitches.

Join a hand to the lower edge of a pink arm, in the position shown on the diagram, matching X's. Join another hand to a mauve arm, in the same position, but stitching on the opposite side, so that, when matched together, the stitching on both arm pieces will be on the outside. Now place together and oversew all round the hand, using flesh-coloured cotton. Stuff the hand lightly. Join remainder of lower edge of sleeve, and the sides, in black, leaving open between the notches. Stuff the arm (not too much in the lower point of the

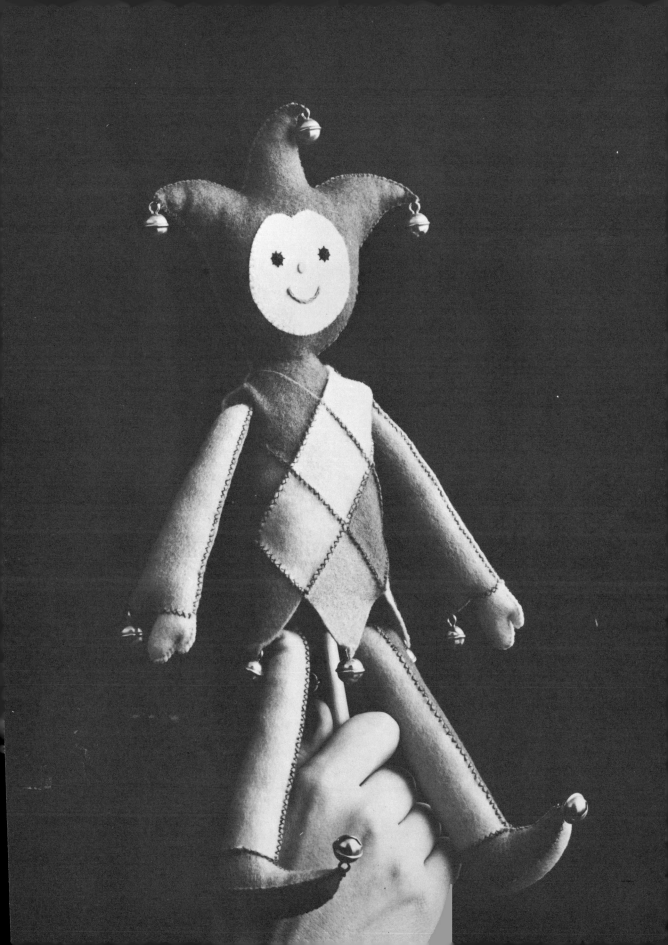

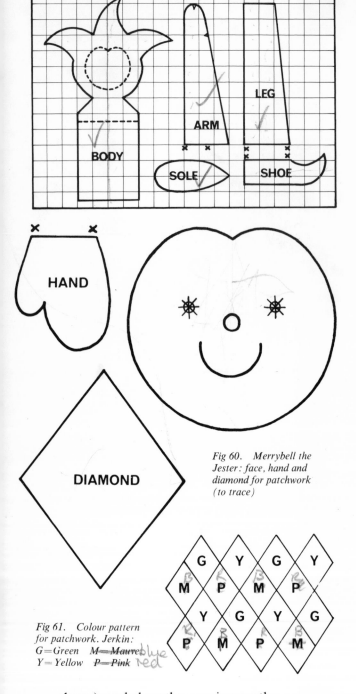

Fig 59.   Merrybell the Jester: body. One square=½in.

LEG

ARM

BODY

SOLE

SHOE

HAND

DIAMOND

Fig 60.   Merrybell the Jester: face, hand and diamond for patchwork (to trace)

G	Y	G	Y
M	P	M	P
Y	G	Y	G
P	M	P	M

Fig 61.   Colour pattern for patchwork. Jerkin: G=Green   M=Mauve Y=Yellow   P=Pink

front and back seams of the shoe. Then stitch a sole into position, matching the centre back and front point to the seams. Stuff the foot. Stitch the two sides of the leg together, leaving open at the top. Complete stuffing the leg, then fold together so that the seams match at the centre, and stitch straight along the top.

Make the second arm and leg *exactly the same* as the first.

Trace the face on to a piece of tissue paper: tack this into position on the felt face. Embroider the mouth, in stem stitch, through the paper, and mark the position of the nose and eyes. Cut the nose in deep pink felt, or embroider it, and cut the eyes in black felt (use the largest size hole on a leather punch, if you have one). Stitch or stick the eyes lightly into position, then embroider a star in long straight stitches as indicated on the pattern, using black double cotton. Stitch or stick the nose into position (if felt). Then appliqué the face to the right side of the green body, as indicated on the pattern.

Stick buckram lightly into place on the wrong side of the yellow felt (or tack). Wrong sides together, join the green and yellow body pieces all round the head, leaving open below the broken line. Stuff the head (buckram flat at the back), pushing well up into the points of the hat. Now join the sides, and stuff the body, inserting the spoon, and stuffing firmly round it, as you do so. Close the lower edge, the spoon's handle protruding in the centre, and stitch the tops of the legs to the lower edge of the body at each side of the spoon.

Stitch tops of arms securely to each side of the body at the lowest point of the shoulder (thumbs facing forward).

Stitch the patchwork diamonds together as for the body, arranging the colours as indicated in the diagram. Press on the wrong side, under a damp cloth, then join to form a "tube" and press the join. Fit the jerkin on the body and catch the top diamonds together on each shoulder, as illustrated.

Stitch bells at points of hat, sleeves, jerkin and toes.

sleeve), and close the opening neatly.

Stitch a pink shoe piece to a green leg, positioning as shown, matching X's. Join a mauve shoe to a yellow leg in the same way, but stitching on the opposite side, as for the hand and arm. Place together, and join the